CRYSTAL SKULLS

Interacting with a Phenomenon

Jaap van Etten, PhD

CRYSTAL SKULLS

Interacting with a Phenomenon

Jaap Van Etten, PhD

Light Technology Publishing

Photo Credits

Mitchell-Hedges Skull Photo: Cover and Plate 1 Color Photograph, page 167;
A Frank Dorland Photo, © Vandria Rayner-Dorland.
For permission to utilize the Frank Dorland photographs, please inquire to
Mrs. Vandria Rayner-Dorland, PO Box 6233, Los Osos, CA 93412-6233,
or by email to vrdorland@aol.com.

Sam Photo: © Amayra Hamilton.

Nebula Photo: © NASA and the Hubble Heritage Team (STScI/Aura)

ISBN-10   1-891824-64-3
ISBN-13   978-1891824647

Published by

800-450-0985
www.lighttechnology.com

PO Box 3540
Flagstaff, AZ 86003

Dedication

This book is dedicated to my beloved wife, Jeanne Michaels. She has stimulated me over and over to deepen my connection with the crystal skulls. We have been exploring crystal skulls for nine years. Without her abilities, qualities and deep connection with crystals and crystal skulls, this book would never have been written.

Acknowledgments

No book can be written without the support of other people. Many have contributed in small or more significant ways to the information contained in this book. Some I have forgotten the names of, because they only were there for a short moment. Others have been there for longer periods or still are contributing to my ongoing journey with the crystals skulls. I would like to thank everyone who has been part of my crystal skull adventure.

In addition to the many who have contributed in a more general way, there are those whose contributions I would like to mention in a more personal way. First I would like to thank Amayra Hamilton. You have been on my crystal skull journey from the beginning, starting in Holland, until today. We have stimulated each other in different phases, helping each other to grow in understanding of what crystal skulls are. You encouraged me in writing this book and contributed in many ways to it. You took most of the photos and your editing skills have greatly improved its readability.

Michael Hamilton, you simply are always there for me. In that way, you have supported, challenged and stimulated me on my journey. Your friendship is deeply valued.

Joe and MaryLee Swanson—many of our special crystal skulls came from you, especially in the initial phase, when we began to build up our crystal skull family. Our discussions have contributed to my understanding of the crystal skulls and of the people connected with them.

Eric and Susan Youngman were always able to bring interesting crystal skulls into our lives. You often made us forget that "we did not need more skulls," and in that way, you have largely contributed to the formation of a wonderful and special group of crystal skulls.

Joshua Shapiro—I met you initially through emails and for the first time in 1999 in Las Vegas. Our paths have crossed each other many times, and our meetings have always been stimulating.

Mary-Ann Mathot, you organized several workshops on crystal skulls and crystals in Holland. We have stayed in contact for many years, sharing our enthusiasm for crystals and crystal skulls.

Additionally, I want to thank Joyha Baker, who made almost all the drawings in this book and contributed to the editing. I also would like to thank Dhee A. Koenig for the wonderful design of the cover.

I would also like to thank the caretakers of old and ancient skulls that I met on my journey. Some of the caretakers and their skull(s) have had a significant impact on my understanding of crystal skulls, namely JoAnn Parks, Joky van Dieten, Frank Loo, Sherry Whitfield and several others I met only briefly or who do not want to be mentioned.

For all the people who have participated in our crystal skull meditation evenings, I would like to thank you for the enthusiasm, feedback and support. I would especially like to thank Gary Palisch and Sandra O'Connor, who gave the impulse to start these meditations. I also want to mention those who have been our regulars—Sandra O'Connor, Gary Palisch, Amayra Hamilton and Joyha Baker—as well as those who have been frequent participants—Cher Lynn, Thelma Moeran, Elizabeth Keller, Donna Bius, Diana Rodriguez, Catherine Kubu and Rebecca Kilawee.

I would like to thank Melody Swanson, publisher of Light Technology Publishing, and her staff for the creation of the final product, the book as it is. Thank you for your trust in me that led to the publishing of this book. I would also like to thank the staff for their contributions, especially Laura Monroe for her invaluable final editing.

Lastly I would like to thank the person who has had the strongest influence and made the largest contribution to my crystal skull journey: my beloved wife, Jeanne Michaels. My love, without you I would never be where I am now. You have stimulated me when I needed stimulation. You have supported me when I needed support. You have reconnected me with the crystal skulls when I tended to move away from them. We have done so much work together which helped me to gather the insights and knowledge that have led to the writing of this book. Your editing, your questions and your advice have been invaluable. I want to thank you from the depths of my heart.

Table of Contents

Introduction

In 1994, I visited the Four Corners area in the Southwest of the United States for the first time. I was then still living in my home country of Holland. Over the course of our one month visit, my wife at that time, Carina, and I stayed in Sedona for eleven days. During our stay we visited many metaphysical bookstores. For a reason I did not understand at the time, I was strongly attracted to the books of Lazaris (channeled by Jach Pursel). I ended up buying two of the three books that were available, but I could not find the third book. Instead of being happy with the two books, I felt a strong urge to also get the third. Every day I tried to find that third book—it came close to a compulsion. I had almost given up when on the last day before our departure, I talked to someone at one of the New Age centers. He told me there was a woman who privately sold the Lazaris material. I was lucky: She was at home, she was willing to see us and she had the book I wanted so badly.

In addition to the Lazaris material, this woman, Lin, had a large collection of crystals in her house. At the time I already had a strong interest in crystals, so it was exciting to look at her collection. At a certain moment, she looked at me and asked me to sit down and close my eyes—she had something she wanted me to experience. I felt a bit silly, sitting there with my eyes closed, but at the same time, I felt an expectation similar to that of a child about to unwrap his Christmas present. I heard her coming back into the room and I suddenly felt a heavy cold smooth stone in my hands. Without even knowing what it was that I held, I started to cry. I had no clue why I was crying, and I still had not opened my eyes. I then heard Lin say to Carina: "This has happened several times before."

After sobbing for about half an hour, I was ready to open my eyes. I was sitting with a crystal skull in my hands. I had never heard of crystal skulls, let alone seen one. I did not understand why somebody would want to make a skull out of this beautiful crystal. Finally I was able to ask some questions. It turned out that I was sitting with a contemporary skull carved a couple of years earlier by a Japanese carver. Lin was only a temporary caretaker of this crystal skull she called Ted. She told us she had seen strange things happening around the skull, including spontaneous healing. Her stories only increased my confusion.

I left Sedona with the three bosddoks of Lazaris in my suitcase. To this day I have not read them; I have actually given them away. I did not go to Lin's house because of the Lazaris book—I went there to meet my first crystal skull. The books were the way my guidance got me to the right place to make my first contact with crystal skulls.

I went home with many questions in mind. Why had I reacted the way I did? What were crystal skulls? Like many people, I grew up in a society that associated a skull with death. However, what I had felt had nothing to do with death. On the contrary, I felt very much alive when I connected with the skull. I later learned that there are societies where the skull is the symbol of knowledge and wisdom. It was that aspect I connected with when I held the crystal skull in Sedona. It was an unconscious recognition of what the crystal skull stood for: wisdom, knowledge and consciousness.

My experience in Sedona started a personal search into the meaning of crystal skulls. It also induced a longing to have my own crystal skull to work with so I could study and experience this phenomenon. It took me two years to get a human-sized clear quartz crystal skull called Sam that was carved in Brazil on my special request [see Fig. 1]. That started a period of research and of experiencing crystal skull energies. My current wife, Jeanne, and I now have one small ancient crystal skull (carved more than fifteen hundred years ago), two small old crystal skulls (carved between one hundred and fifteen hundred

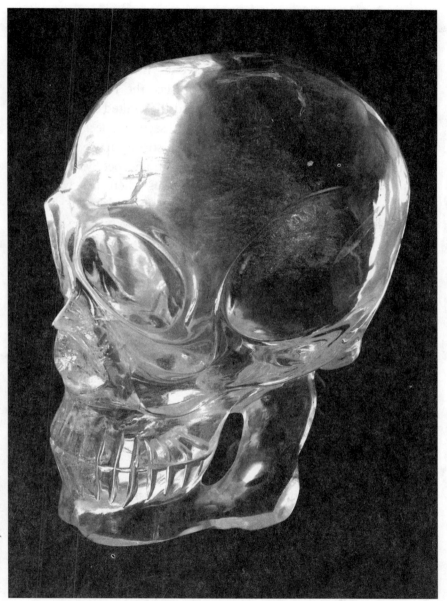

Photo © Amayra Hamilton

Fig. 1. Sam, the author's personal favorite fully activated contemporary clear quartz crystal skull.

years ago) and more than one hundred and twenty contemporary crystal skulls of different sizes carved from different types of crystals

Until the mid-1990s, crystal skulls were a rare phenomenon. Not many people had the opportunity to see one. If they had, it was most likely the Mitchell-Hedges crystal skull or Max, the Texas crystal skull. The Mitchell-Hedges Skull traveled around the United States until the beginning of the 1990s, where it could be seen in special gatherings and at metaphysical fairs. This crystal skull stirred up people's imaginations. Many stories have been told about it, and people reported all kinds of strange phenomenon and experiences when they were in its presence. Max, like the Mitchell-Hedges, is an ancient crystal skull that has traveled many places in the United States. While the Mitchell-Hedges crystal skull was "in hiding" due to the health of its caretaker Anna Mitchell-Hedges, Max, with its caretaker JoAnn Parks, traveled almost every weekend in the United States and to Europe as well. This does not change the fact that, at the time, connecting with a crystal skull was still a rather rare opportunity.

This changed around the mid-1990s. A large number of contemporary crystal skulls became available as peoples' interest grew. Soon the number of people who were caretakers of one or more contemporary crystals skulls began to increase. When a person makes a deep connection with crystal skulls, he or she usually becomes the caretaker of more than one. The person feels so attracted to them that before he or she realizes it, he or she has built up quite a collection [see Plate 10 and Plate 20].

Many wonder what kind of person has this strange attraction to crystal skulls. Are these people connected to death? Do they belong to a strange cult? When meeting these "crystal-skull people," it soon becomes clear that neither is true. I, my wife and our many friends who have connected with crystal skulls are intelligent people with sound minds. So what is so special about crystal skulls that people feel attracted to them? This question is especially relevant because the attraction is often very strong.

My story turns out to be in no way unique. I have heard many similar stories of a deep first contact, leading to a search for the meaning of crystal skulls. This book is a reflection of my search for that deeper meaning.

This book is not meant to duplicate existing books. There are some very interesting and informative books written, such as *Mysteries of the Crystal Skulls Revealed*, by Sandra Bowen, Nick Nocerino and Joshua Shapiro, and *The Mystery of the Crystal Skulls: Unlocking the Secrets of the Past, Present, and Future*, by Chris Morton and Ceri Thomas—both which are considered the most informative books on the subject at this moment. Although this book contains general information that you might find in other books, its purpose is to summarize different aspects of crystal skulls in a new way, adding new discoveries as well. The information in the book will help us to see that crystal skulls are one of the most amazing gifts to humankind. It will show that crystal skulls help us to explore many aspects of our awareness and expanding consciousness, and of our interaction with the Earth and the universe. Crystal skulls invite us in different ways to embark on a journey that leads to a deeper understanding of who we are.

This book has four parts. Part One describes the characteristics of crystal skulls from a physical and metaphysical point of view. Crystals, the shape of skulls and the qualities of crystal skulls and crystals are also discussed. Different types of crystal skulls are defined, and some of the known old and ancient crystal skulls are described. Part Two focuses on different energetic aspects of crystal skulls and on the effect crystal skulls have on human beings. Finally, Part Three describes the legend of the thirteen crystal skulls as well as a description of the author's personal exploration of this legend.

To a certain degree, crystal skulls are an enigma. From a scientific point of view, they are no more than a crystal in the shape of a skull, or "an interesting archaeological find." However, this is not the way people who connect with crystal skulls experience them. They experience them as special and as wonderful tools that awaken something in themselves. Experiencing strange phenomenon while connecting with crystal skulls, especially ancient ones, is common. From a scientific viewpoint, these experiences can lead to statements such as "fraud" and "unsubstantiated claims." This response is not unique. We see similar responses with phenomena like crop circles, UFO sightings, alternative healing modalities, dowsing and other scientifically "unexplainable" phenomena.

However, this does not diminish many peoples' interest in these subjects. Actually, interest is increasing. Hard science seems to be losing its power. Science is no longer seen as the complete way to view our world. Alternative views have become more acceptable, and there is an increase in the value of a spiritual approach so that what you feel has a valuable place in understanding who you are. Besides the mind (science/logic), feeling (experience/illogic) now has value. Experiences, though subjective, have more value than science would like us to believe. The value of experiences also stems from quantum physics that tells us that as observers we have an influence on reality. In other words, we create our own reality.

Only through our personal experiences can we understand what we need to believe in order to create the reality we experience. Our experiences reflect our state of mind, our belief structures and our emotions. We learn from our experiences and can decide whether we like or dislike them. By looking at our belief structures, we are able to understand what we need to change in order to create the reality we want. Crystal skulls can help us in this process and are therefore valuable friends. Crystal skulls can help us to connect with knowledge and to deepen our experiences. This leads to a deeper understanding of who we are, as understanding comes from a combination of information, knowledge and experience.

Accepting that experiences are essential for understanding the phenomenon of crystal skulls does not mean that we should accept every experience as the truth. Each experience and the ideas connected with it are true for the person who has the experience. That does not mean that this is also true for others. Experiences have value when we share them and are able to see the common patterns that emerge. For this reason, it is important that the caretakers of crystal skulls work together and honor each other's beliefs and experiences.

However, the crystal-skull world reflects the larger human world in many ways. There can be a lot of competition. Certain skulls are considered "better" because they are considered older. Caretakers who claim to have an ancient crystal skull may be seen by others as frauds. It is important to realize that crystal skulls may reflect and reinforce what is already present, including criticism and jealousy.

In this book, I describe crystal skulls and their age as they are generally accepted. However, I also show that it is not important whether a crystal skull is ancient, old or new, and offer a new way of categorizing crystal-skull groups. The energies and information contained in crystal skulls are not necessarily based on the age of crystal skulls. In addition, nobody knows for sure how long ago a certain crystal skull was carved.

Each crystal skull has its own unique function as part of the whole. If we are open, each skull can teach us something. The function of the contemporary crystal skulls is more important than most people realize. This book will explore these different aspects without prejudice or judgment. Every experience has value. We are all still students in the understanding of crystal skulls. If there are any masters on the subject, they have not yet revealed themselves. Even being a caretaker of an ancient skull does not guarantee that we have mastered the subject.

In conclusion, I invite you to read this book with an open mind. Some scientific elements are included, but this is not a scientific book. It reflects a study in which mind and feeling, knowing and experiencing, and the masculine and the feminine approach work together to come to a deeper understanding of a subject that intrigues an increasing number of people. Following the explorations of the author as presented in this book may open the door for you to find your own way in the exploration of the phenomenon of crystal skulls. If you enter it with an open mind and an open heart without expectations or judgment, taking in what you resonate with and leaving alone what you don't connect with in the moment, you will experience their amazing value.

Overview

I n the following chapters, I will present several ideas about crystal skulls. Some of them are generally accepted; others may sound new or even like pure fantasy. A subject like crystal skulls would never lead to a satisfying publication if we restricted it to hard scientific facts. Crystal skulls and their attraction for an increasing number of people cannot be explained by scientific facts. They cannot be explained at all. They can only be understood if we allow ourselves to go into the area of experiences, sensing and feeling.

This does not give us "evidence" that falls within the current scientific paradigms, but it leads to an interaction with crystal skulls that gives us unique experiences. Since there is no "hard evidence," you, the reader of this book, are completely free to do with the information whatever you want. You can shrug your shoulders, you can see it as an interesting story of the writer, or you can use it as an invitation for your interaction with the crystal skulls.

Crystal skulls have all the characteristics of crystals. However, from an energetic point of view, the crystal skulls become "different" as soon as the shape of a crystal skull appears as it is being carved. When the crystal skull shape appears, the energy shifts in frequency. Due to this frequency shift, the crystalline structure moves from the collective crystal energy field into the collective crystal skull energy field. This field holds the energies of all crystal skulls, whether they are original, singing, fully activated (old and ancient) or contemporary skulls. Each crystal skull contributes in its own unique way to this collective field in the same way as each human contributes to the collective consciousness field of humankind.

Crystal skulls help us to expand our consciousness. They help us to connect with what we feel about ourselves and what we think about ourselves. This means they help us to see what our beliefs about ourselves truly are. This allows us to make decisions to change what we would like to change and to keep what we like about ourselves and our beliefs. Crystal skulls also help us to connect with other-dimensional aspects of ourselves. We are multidimensional beings, and crystal skulls can help us to connect with other-dimensional aspects as far as it is relevant for understanding and expressing who we are.

There is a certain hierarchy among crystal skulls. This is not a hierarchy that indicates which crystal skull is more important than another, but it is a functional hierarchy. Crystal skulls created in the different phases of humankind's involution have different functions in the phase of evolution. The importance of all crystal skulls is clear when we understand this evolutionary process and the role crystal skulls can play in it.

There are crystal skulls that are called the *original crystal skulls*. They consist of twelve groups, each having three crystal skulls. In addition, there is a central skull, which makes the total number thirty-six plus the central skull. The original crystal skulls contain information to help shift humankind's consciousness. These skulls are not yet present in the physical world, and most likely they never will be.

To connect and work with the crystal skulls in a physical way, the Atlanteans created the *singing crystal skulls*. They created a total of fifty-two crystal skulls: four groups of thirteen. I believe they did not carve them but had mastered the process of morphocrystallic generation and morphocrystallic transformation. Either their consciousness created a matrix (morphocrystallic generation) or through intent they used a human skull as the matrix (morphocrystallic transformation) to create the crystal skulls. I believe the Mitchell-Hedges crystal skull was created through morphocrystallic transformation.[1]

After the destruction of Atlantis, people went to different places all over the world and they took the singing crystal skulls with them. My sensing is that there are still thirty-one of them around, but they no longer form groups of thirteen. I believe that several of these crystal skulls will surface to help us to expand our ability to connect with them.

This will ultimately lead to an interaction and connection with the original crystal skulls.

Once they were settled in their new locations, the survivors of Atlantis began to carve crystal skulls. They carved them in order to stay connected to the information field of the original crystal skulls, hoping to re-create a highly developed civilization that would move into a golden new age. The carving of crystal skulls has actually never stopped and continues today with the carving of the *contemporary crystal skulls*.

Due to the process of involution, the knowledge of how to create crystal skulls that are fully functional and optimally connected with the collective crystal skull field got lost. Also, the knowledge of how to use the crystal skulls was lost over time, or at least to a large degree. We see this reflected in the contemporary crystal skulls. Once carved, the crystal skulls are barely activated—that becomes the task of the caretakers. They are the ones that have started the process of evolution, which will eventually lead to the connection of all crystal skulls on all levels. This will allow us to use the information stored in them to create a new time in which we again understand who we truly are.

I believe that the legend of the 12 + 1 crystal skulls has a basis of truth. There are portals through which the original crystal skulls have come to Earth, but these portals are no longer fully activated. The understanding of how to activate these portals may be the answer to the question of how to access the information given by beings with a different consciousness to Earth through these original skulls. It may even be possible that the original crystal skulls are the portals themselves. In a channeling, Bashar, a multidimensional being who speaks through channel Darryl Anka, called crystal skulls doorways to other dimensions.[2]

Crystal skulls also have a healing function. This has been described by many people. I believe that healing (which means becoming whole) takes place through awareness and expanding consciousness. That may be the reason why crystal skulls are such good healers: they expand our consciousness and help us to see ourselves, allowing for conscious or unconscious change.

I believe that contemporary skulls ultimately can do what all ancient and old skulls can do. However, it requires growth and understanding from the caretakers to allow this to happen. I believe that the process will go quickly in the coming years.

In this book, we will look at many aspects of crystal skulls. In some ways, we seem to know a lot about them, but on the other hand, there is even far more that we do not know. We are in a phase of exploring many spiritual tools, and crystal skulls are one of them. These explorations are important because they help us to see who we are.

PART 1

Uhat Is a Crystal Skull?

Crystal skulls are carved from crystals, either recently or in ancient times. This means that each crystal skull, besides having the characteristics of a crystal skull, also will have the characteristics of the crystal it is carved from. In this context, crystals can be a singular crystalline structure (i.e., clear quartz) or a mixture of crystalline structures (lapis lazuli, ruby in zoisite and others). For that reason, we will look first at crystals in general and then at the characteristics that crystals and crystal skulls have in common. Next we will look at the skull shape, summarize information on most of the known old and ancient skulls, and then finally look at some aspects of contemporary crystal skulls.

CHAPTER 1

Characteristics of Crystal Skulls

All crystals have been created through processes in the Earth and thus are an intrinsic part of the Earth. When we buy a crystal in a shop, we may not always connect with the awareness that we are actually buying a piece of the Earth that has been taken from her. We are so separate from the Earth that we think nothing about what it means for her to be mined or for the crystal to be ripped apart from her.

When a crystal is taken from a mine, we literally disconnect the crystal from its source. As long as a crystal is in the Earth, there is a direct connection and a free exchange of energy and information between the crystal and its natural environment. When we take the crystal out of that environment, it will no longer have that direct connection, nor will it have that exchange of energy. When we fully realize what happens to a crystal, we may be more grateful for the gifts that crystals bring and treat them with gratitude and deep respect. Crystals are a wonderful gift of the Earth to help us to understand who we are. What that means in the author's opinion will become clearer as you read this book.

Everything Has Consciousness

Remembering that a crystal has been a part of the Earth may help us to understand the beliefs of many Native traditions. They believe that stones and crystals contain information of the Earth's history. Crystals can give us this information if we learn how to listen to the messages that are stored in them. Listening to the stories of the Earth helps us to reconnect with her.

The Earth is truly our mother who nurtures and supports our physical system—our physical body with its connected energy systems like meridians and chakras—in an optimal way. People tend to forget that we cannot complete our spiritual journey if we do not also fully embrace our physical system. Crystals not only support our spiritual development but also support our connection with this physical system. They help us to recognize the importance of our physical body, because the only way our soul can express itself in this physical reality is through the physical system.

Esoteric teachings and quantum physics help us to accept that everything is and has consciousness and interacts with each other. This means that we relate to and interact with everything that exists. Many people have a special relationship with crystals on a consciousness level. This relationship is important for the understanding of the effects that crystals and crystal skulls have on us. To help the reader to understand this relationship, I would like to give the following description:

> First there was the One. The One was in a state of being that can be described as "Is"-ness. Then the One became self-aware: I am that I am. With this realization, the "I" became explosively the All That Is. The One is in Itself Consciousness. With self-awareness, the Consciousness began to express Itself in an infinite number of ways. One of the ways Consciousness expressed Itself is through the physical world as we know it and what we call our existence.

In order for Consciousness to be able to express Itself in a physical form, It has to lower Its frequencies. The last step before Consciousness manifests in a physical form is called *electromagnetism*. According to Bashar (a multidimensional being who speaks through channel Darryl Anka from what we perceive as the future), the most pure form of solidified electromagnetism is a crystal.[1] That also means that crystals are the purest aspect of consciousness in physical form. Is it then surprising that people who are exploring increasing their awareness and expanding their consciousness are attracted to crystals? (For a clear description and a more scientific point of view of the concept of consciousness and creation, read *Stalking the Wild Pendulum: On the Mechanics of Consciousness* by Itzhak Bentov.)

Many books about crystals mention that crystals affect our consciousness. The best description I have heard about the relationship between crystals and consciousness comes from Bashar. To describe and understand the relationship between crystals and consciousness, I have integrated ideas from Itzhak Bentov, Bashar and my own personal vision. It explains the process of creating physical reality from an energetic point of view, stepping away from religious or scientific evolutionary ideas.

Crystalline Structure and Crystals

The characteristics of crystals are based on the crystalline structure. Each type of crystal has its own defined crystalline structure based on its atomic and molecular structure. For example, many believe that clear quartz is the most important type of crystal for crystal skulls to be made of. The fact that there are so many skulls of other types of crystals and stones indicates that not everybody agrees. However, quartz has certain characteristics that make it one of the best crystals to use for the creation of crystal skulls. Nearly all crystal skulls that are considered ancient are made from quartz. For that reason, the structure of quartz is given as an example

The chemical composition of quartz is SiO_2 (silicon dioxide). When this molecule connects with other SiO_2 molecules, it forms tetrahedrons [see Fig. 2]. A tetrahedron is one of the Platonic solids. Characteristically, for Platonic solids, all faces, all sides and all angles are the same. In the case of a tetrahedron, there are four sides, four faces, and the angles are 60 degrees. In many esoteric traditions, the tetrahedron is seen as the most basic form of the matrix through which all physical forms are created.

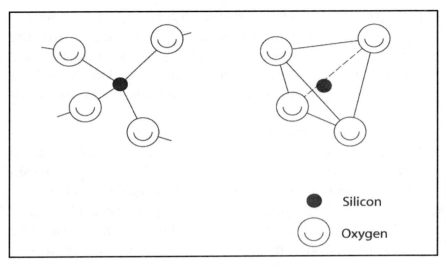

Fig. 2. The molecular structure of silicon dioxide (left), the basic compound for quartz crystals, has the shape of a tetrahedron (right).

In a quartz crystal, the molecules order themselves in a certain way [see Fig. 3]. The ordering results in the physical form of a six-sided crystal. This ordering can be clockwise or counterclockwise around the vertical axis of the crystal. This results in two types of quartz crystals rotating in opposite directions [see Fig. 4]. These molecular characteristics create the crystals that people love so much, but this also forms the basis for their function as a medium for storing information, as we will see later. Every type of crystal has its own chemical composition and atomic matrix, resulting in the many forms, colors and special energies that we enjoy.

The Five Characteristics of Crystals and Crystal Skulls

The characteristics of crystals can be summarized into five different categories. Every crystal and thus every crystal skull has these five char-

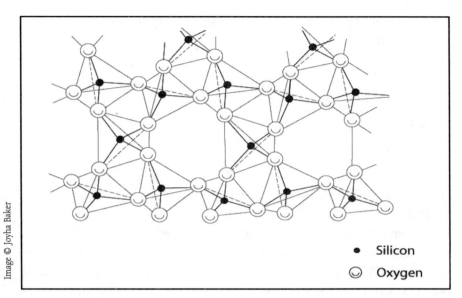

Fig. 3. The molecular structure of quartz.

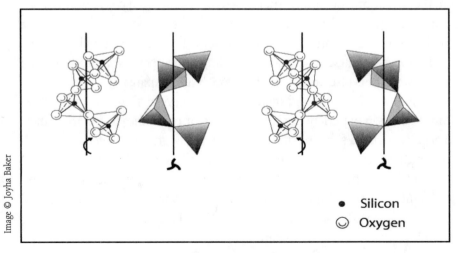

Fig. 4. There are two types of quartz: one in which the tetrahedrons form a spiral that goes clockwise (left), and another in which the tetrahedrons spiral counter-clockwise (right).

acteristics, although the ratio differs for each crystal and crystal skull. Crystals and therefore crystal skulls:

* are reflectors.
* are refractors.
* are transmitters.
* help us to attune.
* store information.

Let us look at these five characteristics in more detail. What do crystals and crystal skulls *reflect* to us? They reflect to us ourselves. They are like a mirror in which we can see ourselves or at least aspects of ourselves. As I just mentioned, crystals can be seen as solidified consciousness. When we connect with crystals and crystal skulls, we connect with consciousness that helps us to see who we are. In this way, crystals reflect aspects not only of our unconsciousness but also of our higher consciousness.

As we will see in Part 2 of this book, crystal skulls and crystals take on the electromagnetic energies of their environment. If the strongest energy in the environment is our energy—which happens typically when we hold the crystal or crystal skull—they will take on aspects of our energy. So by connecting with the crystal or crystal skull, we literally connect with aspects of ourselves. If we are willing to be open to what is reflected to us, we can use this reflection for growth and expansion.

While working with and meditating with crystal skulls, people sometimes mention experiencing past lifetimes or other-dimensional realities. These experiences are related to the characteristic of *refraction*. Like a prism that refracts white light into many colors, crystal skulls and crystals can break the energies of our total system, our total beingness, into different fractions. These fractions may be related to other-dimensional aspects, to past lives or even future lives. This is not a characteristic many people consciously experience.

When we meditate with a crystal skull, we receive a lot of energy (information). Most of this energy/information is received without our being able to translate it into something we can understand. When we do receive images, we may not realize that these images are often symbolic and we are therefore not always able to understand or interpret them. For these reasons, most of the energy connected with the characteristic of refraction is not recognized as such.

Being a *transmitter* means that crystal skulls and crystals are able to receive and send energy/information. This characteristic is widely applied by crystal healers and by those who use crystals to facilitate their healing sessions. They program their crystal, and when they activate the crystal to use it, the information/energy that they programmed into it is "broadcast" by their intention to the intended recipient.

Crystal skulls can also be used by other consciousnesses such as angels or extraterrestrials. They can use crystal skulls to transmit information and/or energy to the crystal skull's caretaker or the person who meditates with the crystal skull. Some people report that they receive messages or even channel information. In order to receive these types of transmissions, we need to relax and be open and receptive to the frequencies that are transmitted. We can attune ourselves as receivers to the "station that is broadcasting."

During the many group meditations with crystal skulls at our home, I have noticed two different transmission systems. In some cases, the beings who use a crystal skull as a transmitter are able to adjust the frequencies so that the recipient can receive the energy/information. The second system is a transmission that sends a defined band of frequencies. The person working with the crystal skull is either able or not to receive (or perceive) that frequency range.

Crystals and crystal skulls also *help us attune*. By meditating with crystals and crystal skulls, we can more easily bring our minds from an active state of awareness (beta) to a more relaxed state (alpha) and then to go even deeper allowing us to go into meditative states (theta and delta). In these deeper states of consciousness, it becomes possible for us to connect with and attune to other beings and consciousnesses.

Many people have a longing to connect with angels, dolphins, beings of light, devas and even with higher extraterrestrial consciousnesses.

Crystal skulls can help us to do that. By holding a crystal skull or by sitting in a crystal skull energy field and setting our intent to connect with or attune to a certain consciousness, the crystal skull's transmitter qualities send out an energetic beacon to that consciousness, inviting it to connect with us. Many beings or consciousnesses are eager to accept this invitation. The angels are a good example of a consciousness that desires to connect with us. Once we are connected with or attuned to the being or consciousness, we may receive a download of information, or energetic transmission.

Every crystal skull has its own range of possible attunements. Certain crystal skulls are very suitable to connect to certain archangels; others are more suitable to attune to extraterrestrial consciousness, and others to devas. Many crystal skulls are even suitable for multiple types of attunements. Only through meditating or working with a crystal skull repeatedly can you explore and discover the many possibilities it has.

The previous four characteristics can only be known through human experience, although there is some measurable evidence that supports the idea of reflection, as we will see in chapter 5. With the last characteristic, the *storing of information*, we find that there are two methods to consider. The technology industry has a deep interest in exploring the possibilities of storing information in crystals. Many people have seen holographic images in movies and Disney theme parks. Using laser technology to create holographic images, it is possible to store a tremendous amount of information in crystals.

Technological applications need artificial crystals (crystals grown in a laboratory under controlled conditions), such as lithium niobate, to minimize the flaws in the crystallization process because these flaws influence the storage and retrieval of information. A piece of crystal the size of a sugar cube can store a whole library of information, yet the technique is still being perfected to ensure accuracy.

Besides the possibility of storing information in a technological way, we can also store information through intent. Our thoughts are electromagnetic frequencies that contain information. Through "setting our intent," this information can be stored in the crystals in a similar way to how lasers store holographic images.

Crystal skulls also seem to take in information from their environment and thus record the history of the place they are located. Many believe that the ancient skulls contain information of ancient times. We are not yet able to access this information, however, most likely because this information was stored by using certain protocols that we do not yet know.

This brings us to an important point: Storing information in a crystal skull is one thing, but retrieving the information is another. The only way to retrieve information from a crystal skull or crystal is by using a similar if not the same system that has been used to program that information. With holographic imaging, this is very clear. The laser that retrieves the information needs to be of the same frequency as the one that programmed it. In the same way, any information in a crystal skull that is programmed with a certain intent needs to be retrieved with a similar intent. Protocols can make the retrieval even more complex.

There is an increasing belief that a lot of information was programmed in crystal skulls using sound and light. We have quite a bit of experimenting to do before we can truly access all information in crystal skulls, especially in those crystal skulls we call ancient. Working with contemporary crystal skulls can help us to develop skills that can help to access the stored information. We will look in later chapters at the role contemporary skulls can play in the expansion of our interaction with crystal skulls in general.

The Skull Shape Opens Us to the Information They Hold

Why do people carve a crystal into a crystal skull? I have been asked that question many times. One reason has to do with the special energies that are connected with crystal skulls (we will look at these energies in the chapters of Part 2). But there are other reasons for using the shape of a skull. The shape is meant to remind us of our own skull. Our skull holds our brain, and our brain processes information. Crystal skulls are believed to hold information, and the shape unconsciously invites us to open ourselves to the information they hold.

In that sense, it is interesting to refer to a Native American saying: "Stones and bones contain all information." The shape of the crystal skull reminds us that the bones of our own skull contain information. Tibetan lamas have been aware of this, and certain monasteries keep the skulls of the lamas who had lived in the monasteries on shelves in rooms. Whenever they are in need of information that they do not have readily available, they visit these rooms. Some lamas meditate, whereas others produce sounds. Through the sounds, the information is unlocked from the skulls and the meditating lamas are able to retrieve it. More generally, it seems that sound is able to unlock information that is stored in systems with a certain molecular structure. According to some people, sounds can be used to unlock information that is contained in the crystal skulls.

The skull shape acts as a reminder, both of the fact that there is information stored and that we need to use our own head and brains to discover ways to access this information. Perhaps the shape tells us that only when our brain works in resonance with the information stored in the crystal skulls will we be able to access this information.

The skull may remind us of death and decay, which our culture often views in a negative or fearful way. But death also represents change, transformation, an opportunity to pass into another dimension. Similarly the crystal skull acts as a doorway into other dimensions. (We will look at crystal skulls as doorways in more detail in chapter 7 in the section about Bashar.)

CHAPTER 2

Categorizing Crystal Skulls

ost people working with crystal skulls tend to categorize them into three groups: ancient, old and contemporary. I prefer to categorize them differently. However, since the terms "contemporary," "old" and "ancient" are commonly used, I will describe these terms. Then I will describe the categorization system I prefer, which separates crystal skulls into *four* categories, and I will explain why I have this preference.

The Ancient, the Old and the Contemporary

Contemporary crystal skulls are considered to be carved within the past hundred years. *Old crystal skulls* are those that have been carved between one hundred and fifteen hundred years ago. Finally, *ancient crystal skulls* are those that were carved more than fifteen hundred years ago. Joshua Shapiro, who is at the moment one of the most active crystal skull researchers, uses these definitions.[1] They were also used on the website for the Crystal Skull Festival in the Netherlands in 2006, for which Joshua Shapiro was one of the main organizers.[2]

As clear as these definitions might seem to be, there is no scientific method that can determine when a crystal skull was carved. Crystalline material and stones are by definition ancient and may be millions of years old. So when we talk about the age of a crystal skull, we mean the period of time that it has existed in the form of a crystal skull. One way we can estimate a probable age is through the clues provided by the anthropological location where they were found. However, a crystal skull may be much older than the ruins, graves or other locations where they were discovered. Another way of estimating age is by looking at whether modern tools were used for the carving of the skull. When tool marks are found, most people believe that we are dealing with an old or contemporary skull. This may be true; however, a skull may have been reworked to make it more esthetically appealing to increase its value.

Skulls that do not have tool marks are considered ancient. Again, this is not necessarily true. Nowadays, carvers are so skilled that they are able to fake an ancient crystal skull. When we decide to accept that a crystal skull is ancient, we do not have any scientific techniques that can tell us exactly when it was carved. In summary, we currently have no way of verifying with absolute certainty how old a crystal skull is.

In many cases, psychics "feel" into crystal skulls and provide a guess of a time frame. When several psychics independently define the same time frame, the label given is generally accepted. My wife Jeanne and I have one small skull that we consider to be old (around 750 years) and one that could just be considered ancient (1700 years) [see Plate 8]. Of course, we do not know this for sure. These estimations of age are based on what we perceived and what several psychics sensed.

Whenever we psychically sense into the age of crystal skulls, we may want to take into account the information that Bashar has passed on through his channel Darryl Anka. Bashar comments that due to the specific matrix that underlies the form of crystal skulls that connects each crystal skull with the "original model," almost all crystal skulls may feel much older than the date they were physiologically carved.[3] We tend to connect more easily with the ancient "original model" than with the actual age.

The Society of Crystal Skulls International was founded in 1945 by Nick Nocerino. He devoted over fifty years of his life attempting to understand crystal skulls. Nocerino and the Society have been the major authority to determine which crystal skulls are ancient and which ones are not. Over many years, the Society gathered information that has helped in making these determinations. They used different systems of testing, including psychic methods. Unfortunately, a lot of the information the Society has gathered is not available to the public. Since Nocerino died in 2004, it is unlikely that his research will be published soon.

The Four-Group Categorization

After many years of working with crystal skulls, I have concluded that I prefer to use four categories rather than the three just mentioned. The categories that I use are based upon the energies of the crystal skulls rather than on their estimated physical age. Nonetheless, I continue to use the terms "old" and "ancient" because these terms are used in many books and articles.

The first group I call the *original skulls*. (We will look at this group in the chapters of Part 3.) I believe that none of the original crystal skulls exist on Earth in physical form.

The second group I call the *singing crystal skulls*. They are called singing skulls because it is believed that they emit frequencies that can be heard clairaudiently. For that reason, it is said that they "sing." The Mitchell-Hedges crystal skull is in my opinion an example of this group. I believe that all these skulls have a detachable jaw. These skulls were probably the first crystal skulls in physical form and in my opinion were created in Atlantis around twelve thousand or more years ago.

The third group I refer to as the *completely* or *fully activated crystal skulls*. Almost all crystal skulls that are now called ancient or old belong to this group. It seems to me that all the skulls referred to as "ancient" were made after the destruction of Atlantis. In my opinion, several groups of thirteen crystal skulls but also many individual skulls were carved to allow the scattered Atlantean groups of people to store and access the knowledge of the Atlantean world. I believe they stored the information from the Atlantean civilization in order to have a record of their past knowledge. However, by the time these crystal skulls were carved, much of that knowledge had already been lost.

I believe the crystal skulls that are considered ancient require that some kind of protocol be used to retrieve the information. The protocol acts like a kind of password. This was probably done to protect the information that was downloaded into the crystal skulls but also acts as a barrier to us fully understanding them. In order for us to connect with these skulls, we need to know or perhaps to intuit these protocols.

Finally, the fourth group contains the *contemporary crystal skulls*. These are the crystal skulls that have been carved recently and are with few exceptions not yet fully activated. These are the skulls that most of us have available and that we learn with and from. This may give us a foundational experience of crystal skulls in general and prepare us for a deeper connection and understanding of the fully activated (old and ancient) crystal skulls. Ultimately this will help us to access and comprehend the information in the singing and original crystal skulls.

Using the four groups mentioned serves a number of functions. First, it shifts the attention from the current physical approach, which is solely mental and scientific. This approach asks, "Where do they come from? How old are they?"—which brings divisiveness in the crystal skull community. Instead of working together to get a deeper understanding of crystal skulls, often people debate about which crystal skull is oldest, which stories are false, who is right and so on. The issue of age is to a large degree irrelevant for understanding the information that crystal skulls contain. Secondly, this approach allows us to shift our focus to an energetic approach (feeling, experiencing)—"What can they do for us?"—with all the endless possibilities to explore ourselves, to heal ourselves, to gather information and to expand awareness of who we are. Thirdly, this approach offers the crystal skull community the opportunity to work together rather than competing with each other.

In the next two chapters, we will look at some examples of three of these four different groups. (Again, the original skulls will be dis-

cussed in Part 3.) Most of the crystal skulls belonging to the fully activated group and the Mitchell-Hedges Skull can each fill a separate book.
Within the context of this book, I will restrict descriptions to short sum-
maries and refer those who are interested in more information on specific skulls to other sources.

CHAPTER 3

Some Famous Crystal Skulls and Their Caretakers

The Singing Skulls

A Native American legend speaks about twelve or thirteen singing crystal skulls (see chapter 8). I believe that the singing crystal skulls are the first crystal skulls that were physically made on Earth and that the Mitchell-Hedges Skull is one of them. I am aware that some people will not agree with me. However, I invite you to use your discernment to determine whether this skull is energetically different from the other fully activated or ancient skulls. In other words, is the energetic difference between the Mitchell-Hedges Skull and the other ancient crystal skulls greater than the difference between the other skulls within the group of ancient skulls?

The Mitchell-Hedges Skull [see Plate 1] is known to be the most famous ancient crystal skull. It is the subject of several books, has appeared in TV programs, has been featured in many articles, has been subjected to lengthy research and has even become highly controversial.[1] It is a human-sized crystal skull made of clear quartz, weighs 11.7 pounds and is very beautiful. It has a detachable lower jaw, which makes this crystal skull unique [see Fig. 5].

The story goes that the Mitchell-Hedges Skull was discovered on January 1, 1924, in the ruins of a Mayan city called Lubaantun (meaning "place of fallen stones"), during an archaeological expedition led by F.A.

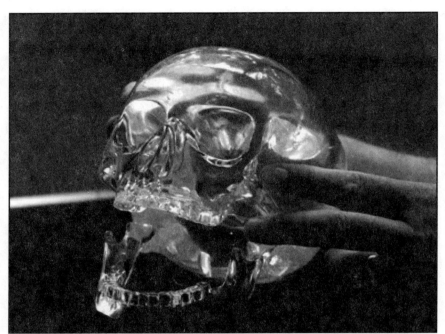

Photo © Amayra Hamilton with permission of Bill Homann

Fig. 5. The Mitchell-Hedges crystal skull, showing the detachable jaw.

Mitchell-Hedges. It was actually his adopted daughter Anna who, according to the story, discovered the skull on her seventeenth birthday. The Mayan people present recognized the skull as a sacred object from their legends and deeply revered it. Mitchell-Hedges decided to give them their sacred object. However, when Mitchell-Hedges left, the Mayans returned the crystal skull to him as a gift to honor all he had done for them.

After the death of Mitchell-Hedges, Anna became the caretaker of the skull and traveled extensively with it, giving many people the opportunity to see and connect with this special crystal skull. She also allowed Frank Dorland, an art conservator and crystal specialist, to study the skull for six years. Dorland's experiences have been summarized in his book *Holy Ice: Bridge to the Subconscious*. The Mitchell-Hedges Skull has amazed many people—in the first place because of the craftsmanship of its carving and secondly because of the effects it has had on people who have been in contact with it.

Joshua Shapiro's e-book, *Journeys of the Crystal Skull Explorers*, contains an interview with Carey Robbins, who is a carver of crystal skulls. He has carved crystal skulls nearly as beautiful as the Mitchell-Hedges Skull, including one with a detachable jaw. He believes that he can produce a copy of the Mitchell-Hedges Skull with one significant difference. Carey knows someone who has spent a lot of time with the Mitchell-Hedges Skull and who is also the caretaker of some of Robbins' own best crystal skull creations. Robbins relates that this person has experienced the Mitchell-Hedges crystal skull "singing" and has seen ancient images in it, and that this has never happened with the skulls Robbins has made.

There have been other skulls similar to the Mitchell-Hedges Skull that have been described. In the late 1940s, near the border of Guatemala and Honduras, Nick Nocerino reported having been shown another crystal skull with a detachable jaw that looked like an exact copy of the Mitchell-Hedges Skull, although it might have been slightly larger. The skull was made of rose quartz and it was carried by a man who might have been a Mayan priest. This report is very reliable, since it came directly from such a renowned researcher. This rose quartz skull has never been seen again—at least there are no other reports of that.[2]

In *The Mystery of the Crystal Skulls*, Morton and Thomas mention that Anna Mitchell-Hedges was approached by a family in Argentina who claimed to have a crystal skull similar to the Mitchell-Hedges Skull. The family reportedly did not want their name known for fear of theft of the skull.[3] Could this be another singing skull?

There are more stories and rumors about crystal skulls with a detachable jaw. Nick Nocerino summarizes some of them in *Mysteries of the Crystal Skulls Revealed*. They all seem to be clear quartz crystal skulls of human size.[4] One is claimed to have been found in the Sierras Madres in Mexico by a group of nine mentalists (mind readers) and their families.[5] I am not surprised by this story, because when I was in that area I kept feeling the powerful presence of one or more crystal skulls (see chapter 8).

Another skull with a detachable jaw is the Zulu Skull, which was stolen from the Zulus. It was as large as the Mitchell-Hedges Skull and was called the Skull of Doom. It was highly revered but also feared. When F.A. Mitchell-Hedges brought the Mitchell-Hedges Skull to Africa, it was initially thought that this was the stolen Skull of Doom. They later realized that this was not the case.[6]

Another crystal skull that supposedly has a detachable jaw is the Berlin Skull. This skull was found by the Gestapo during World War II and was brought to Berlin. It was part of a collection of artifacts and icons with mystical powers that was collected for Hitler's exclusive use. According to Nocerino, the skull was still in Berlin in 1985. It then was moved to Italy (possibly to the Vatican), but it may be back in Berlin.[7]

Nick Nocerino also shares that he has information of a clear quartz, very large crystal skull with a detachable jaw that is somewhere in Peru. It seemed to be in a place called the Valley of the Dead, but Nocerino was not able to find that place when he was in Peru.[8]

Most likely there are more singing skulls, hidden by those who are aware of their power. My belief is that many of them will surface when those who truly understand them connect with them. According to the law of attraction, they will come to those who can match their energy frequencies. Most people who work with crystal skulls do not have that ability yet. As we will see, the fully activated crystal skulls (what we used to call "old" and "ancient" skulls), but also the contemporary skulls, will help us to develop the abilities to attract the singing skulls and ultimately to connect with the original ones.

Fully Activated Skulls (Old and Ancient Crystal Skulls)

Defining a crystal skull as old or ancient can be a sensitive issue for many reasons. The term "fully activated" can shift the focus onto using them as tools in which personal experience is emphasized. Nonetheless, any book on crystal skulls has to give at least some attention to what are known as the old and ancient crystal skulls.

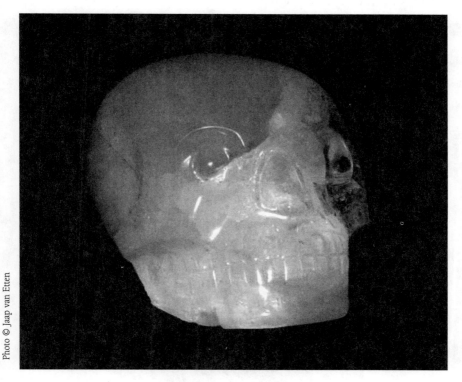

Fig. 6. Max, the Texas crystal skull.

Max: Max is also known as the Texas crystal skull [see Plate 2].[9] It is said that Max, made from clear quartz, was found in Guatemala between 1924 and 1926. The current caretaker, JoAnn Parks, travels extensively with Max, allowing thousands of people to view and experience him. No other caretaker of ancient crystal skulls puts in so much effort to share his or her crystal skull with the world as JoAnn does.

JoAnn and her husband received the skull in 1980 from a Red Hat Tibetan lama named Norbu Chen. This lama received the crystal skull in the early 1970s from a Mayan shaman in Mexico. Norbu Chen, along with his fellow monks, used Max for healing. Max has also been used in many Native American ceremonies.

Max was studied in the British Museum as part of the preparation of a BBC documentary on crystal skulls. Their intent was to prove that the crystal skulls they were testing were not ancient, and they concluded that the crystal skull from their own collection was a recent carving. Interestingly, the researchers did not want to give any conclusions or even comments about Max.[10]

Jeanne and I feel a special relationship with Max. Jeanne describes meeting with Max as meeting with an enlightened master, where she experiences an energy that she describes as love. My experience with Max is that with every meeting something else is awakened in me. These awakenings have helped me to connect deeper with the crystal skulls and have been of great importance to me.

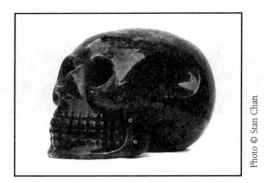

Photo © Stan Chan

Fig. 7. Ami, the Amethyst crystal skull.

Ami (the Amethyst crystal skull): Another ancient skull is Ami, better known as the Amethyst crystal skull.[11] This skull seems to have been part of a collection that was on the desk of President Porfirio Diaz of Mexico sometime between 1876 and 1911. In the year 1911, the Mexican revolution removed President Diaz, and Ami went to the Lascurian family in Mexico. It stayed there until Francisco Reyes, a Mayan priest, purchased the skull in 1979. As an agent for Reyes, John Zamora brought Ami to the United States. In 1983, a group of nine businessmen gave a loan to Zamora. The loan was never repaid, and this group assumed the role of caretaker.

Currently, Ami is for sale for one million dollars. It resides in a vault in California and is rarely displayed, so only a limited number of people have been able to connect with it. It is considered to be a skull for healing and makes a deep impression on those who have seen it. The skull is characterized by a circular indentation at the temples and a white squiggly line that goes around its circumference.

The Mayan Skull: The Mayan Skull is similar in appearance to Ami.[12] This crystal skull is made of clear quartz and has round indentations at the temples similar to Ami. According to the Mayan priest Francisco Reyes—who in 1979 brought both the Mayan Skull and Ami to the United States through his agent John Zamora—the Mayan Skull was found at the Mayan site of Copán, Honduras, in 1912. It was loaned to Nick Nocerino for three months for research. In 1980, John Zamora received a loan from someone in Texas and the Mayan Skull was used as collateral. The loan was never repaid, and the current whereabouts of the Mayan Skull are unknown.

E.T.: The skull E.T. is a smoky quartz skull that was found in 1906 in Guatemala by a Mayan family while digging on their property [see Plate 4].[13] The skull is a little larger than a human skull, with a slightly pointed head and an overbite. In 1991, Joky van Dieten, who lived at that time in Costa Rica, intuitively felt that she needed to call a particular store near Los Angeles to ask for a crystal skull. The store at that time did not have any skulls, but a few days later a crystal skull from Guatemala was offered to them. Joky bought it, became the caretaker and named the skull E.T.

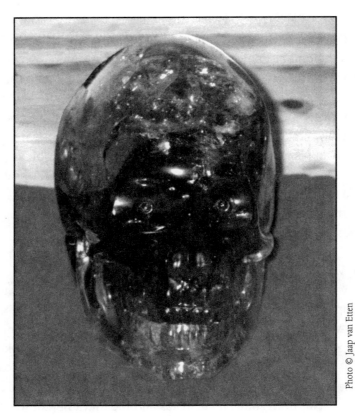

Fig. 8. E.T., a smoky quartz skull.

Joky used E.T. to help her heal from a complex operation in which a large tumor was removed from her head. In May 1999, during a Crystal Skull Conference in Sedona, Arizona, E.T. was acknowledged by Mayan representatives as a lost Mayan skull According to them, E.T. came from the Pleiades. The Mayan representatives confirmed in a sunrise ceremony that Joky was the rightful guardian.

I have met E.T. a couple of times and have been very impressed by this crystal skull. It not only has an alien look but it also *feels* somewhat alien. I had the most powerful experience with E.T. when we met for the first time in 2000. Joky allowed me to position the skulls I had with me around E.T. and create an energy field in which the crystal skulls could exchange energies. Staring intently at E.T., I could see the energy field above the skull opening. It was as if I was watching a science fiction movie. Through the opening (doorway/portal) came a number of beings. They were long and slender, and were radiating light. They positioned themselves around the circle of skulls with E.T. in the center. I was included in the circle and I felt a lot of energy, but I did not receive information I could understand. The experience was so powerful that I completely forgot I was in a room full of people!

ShaNaRa: ShaNaRa is a clear quartz skull that was found in 1995 during an excavation of a Mayan site in the state of Guerrero in Mexico [see Plate 3].[14] Nick Nocerino provided the information as to the location of

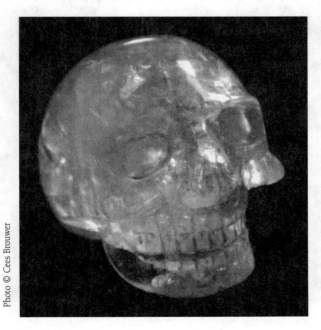

Photo © Cees Brouwer

Fig. 9. ShaNaRa, a clear quartz skull.

what he thought was an ancient temple. Excavation of that location later revealed several carved crystal artifacts, one of which was ShaNaRa.[15] Nick Nocerino was the caretaker until he passed away. Now his wife Khrys and Kirby Seid are the co-caretakers. This skull has been part of many events and was also investigated by the research team of the British Museum. As with Max, no official comment has been given, although unofficially both Max and ShaNaRa are considered ancient skulls.[16]

Rainbow: According to Chuck Pelton, a student of Nick Nocerino, another crystal skull was discovered near the tomb where ShaNaRa was found, which may have been used by the same people.[17] Currently DaEl Walker is the caretaker of this skull, which he calls Rainbow.[18] DaEl,

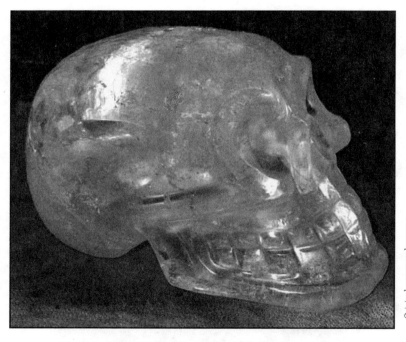

Original source unknown

Fig. 10. Rainbow has been thoroughly studied by the Society of Crystal Skulls International.

however, seems to have a different history: "Rainbow came to me three years ago. It was a trade for some other material I had. The trader said it came down to him from his Grandfather and was given to him by two priests from Guatemala. I have not been able to verify this."[19] Are these variations of the same story? The skull has been thoroughly studied by the Society of Crystal Skulls International. According to Pelton, it is one of the crystal skulls that seem to have a connection with Atlantis.[20]

Synergy: Sherry Whitfield received the crystal skull Synergy in 2001 as a gift from a European businessman named George [see Plate 5].[21] George acquired Synergy around 1986 to 1987 from a very old native man in a tiny village in the Andes, near the borders of Peru, Bolivia and Chile.

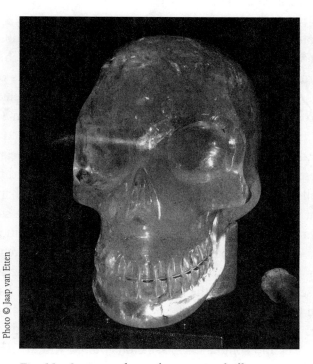

Photo © Jaap van Etten

Fig. 11. Synergy, a large clear quartz skull.

The story goes that when the people of a tribe on a small island in Micronesia saw a picture of the skull, they believed this was the crystal skull that, according to their traditions, was sent in a reed boat from their island to South America. The Micronesians believe that the skull is very old, and based on this, it is believed by some that Synergy originated in Lemuria.

Synergy is a large clear quartz skull. Initially Sherry displayed Synergy in her stores, but now she travels so it can be viewed and experienced by people worldwide at conferences and events, and in private sessions. I met Synergy in the Netherlands in 2006 during the Crystal Skull Festival. There was not much time for a longer personal connection, but in the short moment I was able to touch Synergy, I felt a powerful surge of energy going through my arms and body. It awakened a longing to connect with this skull on a deeper level.

The Himalayan Skulls: I would like to add a group of skulls to the list that is not without controversy: the Himalayan Skulls, which are sometimes referred to as the Beijing Skulls.[22] This group consists of fourteen large skulls, eight small skulls, a nephrite skull and a large meteorite skull. Frank Loo discovered them in caves in the Himalayas in China and brought them to the U.S. People who knew he was interested in ancient artifacts had provided him with information that, over two years, led him to find these artifacts. Along with the crystal skulls, he found three disks that are called Dropa disks. This has led to the conclusion that the skulls are ancient and may have been made by the Dropas. The story of the Dropas seems to be one both of information and misinformation.

The story starts in 1938 with Chi Pu Tei, a professor of archaeology at the Beijing University who went with his students on an expedition to explore a series of caves in the Himalayan Mountains in the Bayan-Kara-Ula area in Qinghai, on the border of China and Tibet. It is believed that these caves were artificially carved. In the caves, they found tombs with short (four feet and some inches) skeletons buried within. These skeletons had abnormally large heads. There were no marks on the graves,

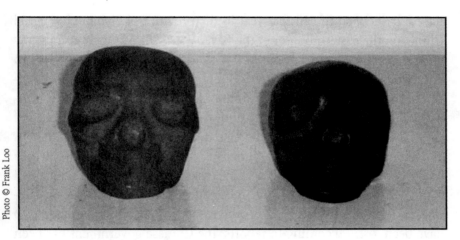

Fig. 12. Two small Himalayan Skulls.

but hundreds of round stones, a foot wide with a hole in the center, were found. The caves also had drawings on the wall. The drawings and the disks were estimated to be about twelve thousand years old.

In 1958, Dr Tsum Um Nui studied the disks and concluded that each groove on the disks contained many small hieroglyphs. When he was able to decipher them, it told the story of a race of extraterrestrials who got stranded on Earth. They lived in these caves, although initially many were killed. He wanted to publish an article but was ridiculed. In 1965, Professor Chi Pu Tei published some information about the alien story.

Russians scientists did research with some of the disks and found an unusually high amount of cobalt and other metallic substances. According to Dr. Vyacheslav Saizev, who described the experiments in the Soviet magazine *Sputnik*, when the disks were placed on a special turntable, they vibrated or hummed in an unusual rhythm as though an electrical charge was passing through them.

In the region where the crystal skulls and the disks were found, there are many stories about little people who used to live in the area. In 1995, a discovery made it possible to believe that these stories could have a basis of truth. In that year in the province of Sichuan in central China, on the eastern border of the Bayan-Kara-Ula Mountains, a pygmy village was discovered. About 120 individuals, ranging from 65 to 115 cm (two feet two inches to three feet ten inches) in height, live a self-sufficient medieval lifestyle. They were unfamiliar with any modern technology. Although the Chinese authorities do not deny the existence of the "Village of the Dwarfs," the village is not open to foreigners.

There is, however, a lot of criticism. Information about the people who discovered the skeletons and the disks seems to be unavailable and is thus not verifiable. Either the information does not exist as some suggest, or it has been destroyed as others believe. Also, the disks seem to have been lost. According to reports, the Chinese government has been collecting the disks to destroy them.

My wife Jeanne and I have been fortunate to meet Frank Loo and see thirteen of the fourteen large skulls. We also saw the three Dropa disks Frank collected. We did private sessions with the thirteen skulls and participated in three ceremonies. Undoubtedly, these crystal skulls have powerful energies.

During one of the crystal skull meditations in our house, we connected with Elizabeth Keller. She brought with her a small crystal skull of which she is the caretaker. Her crystal skull is one of the eight small crystal skulls Frank Loo had collected in the Himalayas. Because Frank Loo got a lot of criticism and received a lot of doubts about the authenticity of the Himalayan crystal skulls, he decided to leave them in the U.S. for sale, and Elizabeth purchased one of them. She calls her skull HeartStar. Elizabeth let this wonderful little skull stay with Jeanne and me several times, which allowed us to connect deeper with it.

During a crystal skull event in Holland in 2006, we met Jeff Krause, who had another small skull of the Himalayan group that he called Apollo 7. He also had one of the large skulls, named Golden Sister of the Moon. Jeff was so kind to let us spend a night with these two Himalayan crystal skulls. Working with these three crystal skulls confirmed our impression that these are not contemporary skulls [see Plate 6].

Photo © Thelma Moeran

Fig. 13. HeartStar, one of the Himalayan crystal skulls.

In 2007, in a personal session with Bashar, I asked whether the Dropas truly existed. He confirmed their existence. On the question whether these beings came from Sirius, as several people believe, he said that was not the case. For some reason, he was not willing to share where they came from. According to Bashar, they are a hybrid race, created through a mixture of human and Gray DNA.[23]

In summary, for us there is no doubt that the Himalayan crystal skulls are powerful crystal skulls that do not feel like recently carved skulls. I can sense that a lot of information is present, but as with all crystal skulls, the protocols to access this information are still unknown.

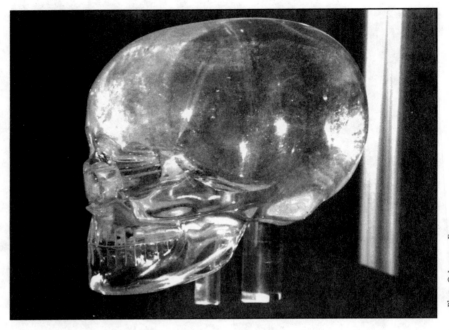

Photo © Jaap van Etten

Fig. 14. The British Skull, also called the Aztec Skull.

The British Crystal Skull: Many people see the British Skull (also called the Aztec Skull) nowadays as old [see Plate 7].[24] Previously it had been considered ancient. This reclassification was based on the fact that some of the teeth of this skull have tool marks, as was demonstrated during research done by the British Museum.[25] However, these tool marks may have been made in a later phase in an attempt to improve the "quality" of the skull and thus its value. This skull, made from a single piece of clear quartz, has been in exhibition in the British

Museum in London, England, since 1898. Probably the skull was acquired by Eugène Boban while he was in Mexico (1862–1867). The skull ended up at Tiffany & Co. in New York, who sold it to the British Museum in 1898 for 120 pounds. The skull is regularly on display in the British Museum and attracts many visitors.

The British Skull was compared with the Mitchell-Hedges Skull in a study that was published in July 1936 in a scientific magazine called *MAN*. The study suggested that the British Skull had dimensions that were very close to those of the Mitchell-Hedges Skull. It has been suggested that the skull could be seen as a simple copy of the Mitchell-Hedges Skull, which does not feel to me to be correct. If the Mitchell-Hedges Skull was the model for the British Skull, it brings up an interesting point. The British Skull, was found earlier than the Mitchell-Hedges Skull, if we are to believe the Lubaantun story. So how could the Mitchell-Hedges Skull have been a model for the British Skull? Or is it coincidence that those two skulls are so similar?

My personal experience with the British Skull has helped me to psychically get an answer to this question for myself. In 1997, I went to the Museum of Mankind in London specifically for the British Museum crystal skull (the crystal skull is now in the British Museum itself and no longer in the department that was called the Museum of Mankind). I spent many hours in front of the showcase the crystal skull was displayed in. The deeper I connected with this crystal skull, the more I was convinced that this was not a recently carved crystal skull, even though tool marks have been found. I strongly felt that this skull was part of one of the groups of thirteen skulls that were carved after the disappearance of Atlantis and that the crystal skulls in this group were separated from each other a long time ago.

I experienced the British crystal skull as a healing skull. This feeling was confirmed when I realized that a pain in my right knee that had been quite serious had disappeared. The same was true for a pain in my lower back. Needless to say, I loved that crystal skull! I also felt that this skull had been used in many different ceremonies. In the ceremonies I could "see," often light was used.

Based on the energies I have felt with this crystal skull and the information I have gathered over time, I believe that this crystal skull was made early after the destruction of Atlantis (see Part 3). Its shape was based on one of the singing crystal skulls. According to the images I saw in my mind's eye when I was with the skull, there were thirteen of these crystal skulls carved to duplicate the crystal skulls that once existed in Atlantis.

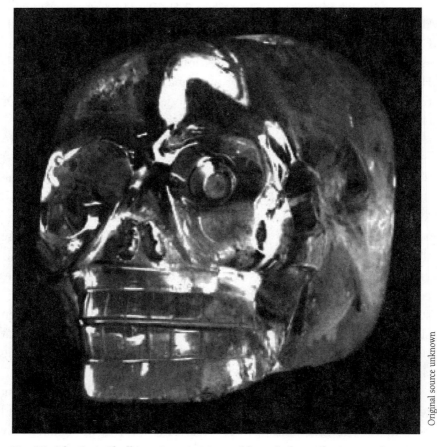

Original source unknown

Fig. 15. The Paris Skull is quite primitive and has a hole cut from top to bottom.

The Paris Skull: According to the generally accepted story, the Paris Skull was also acquired by Eugène Boban at the same time he acquired the British Skull while he was in Mexico.[26] This skull is quite primitive and has a hole cut from top to bottom. It is believed that this hole was made later to hold a Christian cross and that it was not part of the original carving. The Paris Skull is in the collection of the Trocadéro Museum in Paris, France, hence its name. It was purchased from Eugène Boban by Alphonse Pinart, who donated the skull in 1878 to the Musee de l'Homme (Trocadéro Museum). Like the British Skull, this crystal skull is also called the Aztec Skull, but many who have researched the skull believe it to be much older than the Aztec or Mayan civilizations. Chuck Pelton mentions that this skull is believed to be ancient, whereas Joshua Shapiro calls the skull old.[27]

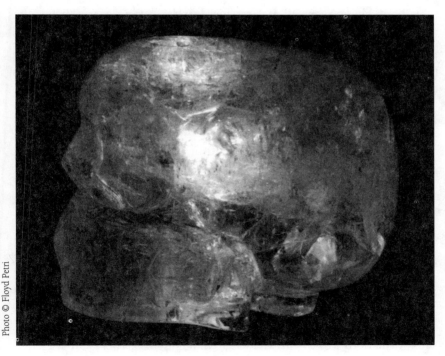

Photo © Floyd Petri

Fig. 16. Windsong, a very primitively carved skull.

Windsong: Another crystal skull that is considered old is Windsong.[28] It is a very primitively carved skull. The current caretaker, Floyd Petri, bought the skull in a crystal store in Austin, Texas. He was attracted to this shop and kept asking for a crystal skull. Finally, the storekeeper gave in and showed Floyd the crystal skull that now is called Windsong. It is a human-sized skull, which, according to various psychics, was carved by a blind craftsman in the 1700s. According to psychics, an extraterrestrial being called Windsong resides inside this skull.

Joky van Dieten and her skulls other than E.T.: In 2001, the crystal skulls that are part of the collection of Joky van Dieten were tested in Austria by Dr. Rudolf Distelberger, a foremost world expert on stones and precious gemstones. Dr. Distelberger did several tests and concluded that Joky's skulls were all at least five hundred years old. That makes them all at least old skulls. In my opinion, they are all ancient crystal skulls that are fully activated. The Jesuit may actually be the youngest of them. Here follows a short description of the other crystal skulls of which Joky van Dieten is the caretaker.

☙ *Baby Luv* is a rose quartz skull that was offered to Joky in March 1993 by a legally appointed executor of wills who had to divide up a Russian estate for underage heirs.[29] The skull had been found in the early 1900s in a burial mound near Lvov (Ukraine) by an old Russian monk. It dates back to the Scythian Age (B.C. 700 to about 330 A.D.). The skull was found lying beside a row of gold art objects for which these Russian steppe people are famous. The monks kept the rose quartz skull for two hundred years before it came into the hands of a Russian family. The monks themselves were convinced that the skull, although used by the Scythians, in reality belonged to the much older Cimmerians. This information ties in with the intuitive feeling that this is an ancient skull.

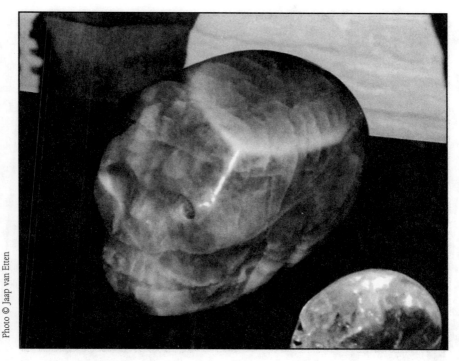

Fig. 17. Baby Luv, a rose quartz crystal skull.

Connecting with this skull was a powerful experience—it was almost intoxicating. I did not receive any information while sitting with this crystal skull. The energies were so wonderful that I came back to it over and over. I feel that it has quite a story to share, but at the time I was unable to move from feeling and enjoying energies into a state of translating what I felt into words. There probably also are protocols in place with this skull, a set of defined steps that seem to have been used when information was programmed in old and ancient crystal skulls.

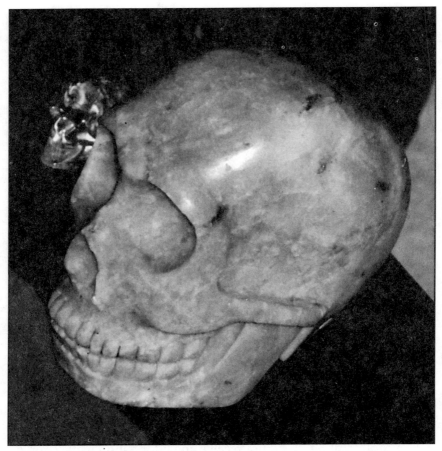

Fig. 18. Shui Ting Er, an amazonite skull.

ง *Shui Ting Er* is an amazonite skull that originated from Southwest
Mongolia, near the Chinese border.[30] It was discovered there 140
years ago by a Chinese archaeologist named Yeng Fo Huu. In the
1930s, a Danish missionary, Pastor Utkielen, was able to buy this
unique skull from the archaeologist's family. Pastor Utkielen's family offered Joky the skull in 1992.

Photo © Joky van Dieten

Fig. 19. The Jesuit, a clear quartz crystal skull.

The *Jesuit* is made of clear quartz crystal.[31] It came into Joky's possession in August 1993, when it was offered to her by the abbot of an American monastery that urgently needed money. It is thought to have a connection with St. Francis of Assisi, who is well-known for his love of animals. The skull has been known since 1534, but it felt to me to be around eighteen hundred years old. According to Joky, this is in alignment with what other people have felt. To me, the Jesuit feels like a healing skull. I love to sit with this skull and to feel how my heart opens. The Jesuit contributes to the healing process of the person who works with it. It also stimulates the healing abilities of the person who connects with it.

Photo © Joky van Dieten

Fig. 20. Mansur, a skull made from lapis lazuli.

❧ *Mansur* is a skull made from lapis lazuli.[32] It was discovered in 1995 in the area of the Amazon rain forest by a north Peruvian Inca tribe. Tuki, the spiritual leader of the tribe, told how they had placed the skull in a cave to cleanse it before handing it over. They were convinced that the skull would be of more benefit to them if they gave it to Joky.

Photo © Joky van Dieten

Fig. 21. Oceana, a skull made from beryl.

❧ **Oceana** is a skull made from beryl.[33] It has the green-blue color of the sea, thus its name. The skull seems to have been passed from one tribe to another, ranging from Peru, Ecuador, Colombia, Brazil and others, before finally coming into the possession of an Indian from a small village in the Brazilian Amazon rain forest. He offered it to Joky in 1997.

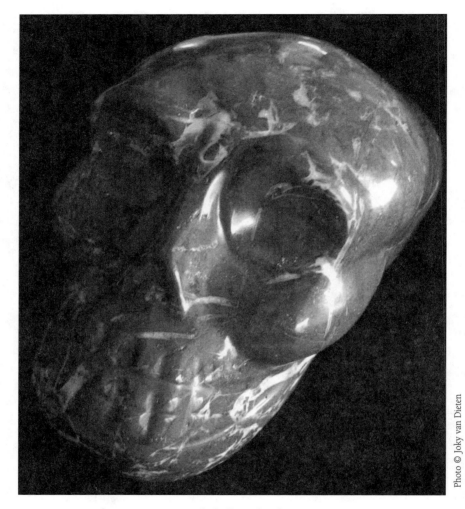

Photo © Joky van Dieten

Fig. 22. Magnificent Fire, a crystal skull made of jasper.

❃ *Magnificent Fire* is a skull made of jasper.[34] It is one of Joky's more recent skulls, acquired in 2002. It was found in Colombia in a cave near the border of Ecuador, close to the Citadel Saphadana near the Rio d'Oro.

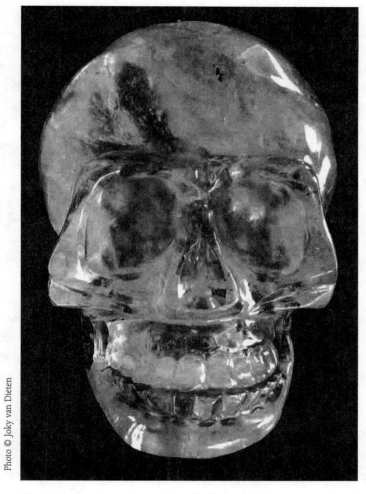

Photo © Joky van Dieten

Fig. 23. Clouds, a clear quartz skull.

~ ***Clouds*** is a clear quartz skull that seems to have been smuggled from a monastery in Nepal.[35] It was bought by Robert Rhodes in 2002. Robert heard of Joky's peace mission, and they both felt that this skull should be part of this mission.[36]

Peru Skull: On his website, Joshua Shapiro reports an interview with Willaru Huayta, a spiritual messenger of the Incas. While traveling in the northern part of Peru, Huayta spent some time with an Indian tribe called the Compas. They started to trust him and one day showed him a crystal skull that was hidden in a cave. The Compa people intuitively knew it was a sacred object, but they did not know what it was used for. They wanted some suggestions from Huayta, but he did not know crystal skulls either. Huayta felt that the crystal skull was used for magnetic healing and contained a very loving energy as well as great wisdom. He felt as if this was a crystallized mind.[37]

This crystal skull is different from the crystal skull in Peru mentioned by Nick Nocerina, listed under the singing skulls.[38] Huayta described the skull as being made from clear quartz with blue in the eyes and on top of the head. The Peru Skull is human-sized and has good workmanship.

El-Aleator and El Za Ra: These two small skulls are 1 1/2 x 2 inches, are made from clear quartz and have some very special characteristics.[39] Susan Isabelle Boynton became the caretaker of these two remarkable little skulls in 2000. She was gifted one when she was in Belize, and a couple of days later she found the other. These two skulls belong together. They have a flat back, and when you put the backs together, they form a perfect human heart shape. They also have a brain that is clearly visible. The energy of these two skulls is very powerful. Susan Isabelle uses the two skulls in her work as a healer, teacher and workshop facilitator.

Ti and Bet: In this list, I want to include two skulls that, although small, are interesting, fully activated skulls. The caretakers are myself and my wife Jeanne. Both skulls were a gift from a friend who bought them in a crystal shop in Pune, India. They were said to come from Tibet. One is made from clear quartz and is called Ti; the smaller one is made from citrine and is called Bet. Ti feels to sensitive people to

Fig. 24. El-Aleator (right) and El Za Ra (left).

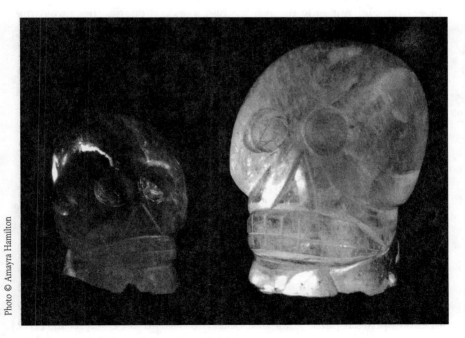

Fig. 25. Ti (on the right) and Bet (left).

be older and is estimated to be around 1700 years old. Bet is believed to be younger than that and is estimated to be around 750 years [see Plate 8].

The images I receive when I meditate with them are quite similar. Both seem to have been used in a shamanic way. They were part of healing ceremonies and were used to charge medicine made from herbs. In more recent times, they have been placed on family altars. The difference between Ti and Bet is not so much how they were used but more by whom they were used. With Ti I have seen and sensed men, whereas with Bet I feel women.

The crystal skulls from Nepal: The last example of fully activated crystal skulls is a group of three rather small crystal skulls that came from Nepal, of which I and my wife are the caretakers. I bought all three skulls from the same seller through eBay. He had more crystal skulls than the three I bought, but only these three had a special energy that raised my curiosity, so I acquired them. When they arrived in April 2007, it was immediately clear that all three were fully activated crystal skulls. However, feeling into their history, they obviously were not very old. A smoky crystal skull of 2.4 inches was estimated to be 114 years old, a clear quartz crystal skull of 1.8 inches to be 76 years old and a clear quartz 3 inch crystal skull to be 87 years old [see Plate 9]. According to the traditional definitions, they would not be considered old.

Meditating with these three crystal skulls gave some interesting impressions. They have been connected with powerful energies. The images I perceived showed that they had been with a group of thirteen crystal skulls. Based on the energies I perceived, this group could have been the group of thirteen singing crystal skulls under the Potala in Tibet (see the chapters of Part 3). All three crystal skulls have been with monks who meditated with them. They used the information downloaded in the little skulls by the singing skulls as a guiding force for their spiritual path. I felt that both the two small crystal skulls have been used by one monk only, whereas the energy connected with the

Fig. 26. Three fully activated crystal skulls from Nepal.

three-inch crystal skull and the images I saw suggested that during a certain period of time several monks used this crystal skull.

I was unable at the time of this writing to perceive any more information. It seems that these three crystal skulls were supposed to have stayed with monks or in monasteries. Why they ended up in two stores in Kathmandu in Nepal I do not know. The seller found them in these two stores and thought they were recently carved like all the others he found.

There is no doubt that the list of the fully activated crystal skulls is much longer. It is obvious that there are far more than thirteen ancient skulls, as some people believe. The style of carving is in most cases very different, and there seems to be no relationship between them. An exception is the similarity between the British Skull and the Mitchell-Hedges Skull. However, I do not consider these two skulls to be part of the same group. There is also a similarity between the Mayan Skull and Ami, the Amethyst Skull. Although it could be possible that several groups of thirteen crystal skulls have been carved in the past, there are at this moment no signs of such groups. It may be possible that the crystals skulls of the different groups are still scattered and possibly they are hidden or have even been destroyed. There are stories that missionaries destroyed crystal skulls because they were seen by the Native people as sacred objects. We will come back to the subject of the thirteen crystal skulls in the chapters of Part 3.

Several other ancient skulls have been reported by reliable sources, but information is insufficient to include them in a small book like this. Slowly information has begun to emerge that there are many ancient skulls hidden by tribal people. However, they choose to protect these sacred objects from the greediness of the white people or, as some say, to prevent the energetic disturbance of these sacred objects due to lack of respect and/or understanding. I am sure that in the near future more ancient crystal skulls will surface.

CHAPTER 4

Contemporary Crystal Skulls and How to Find Yours

Most of the crystal skulls that are available at this moment are contemporary skulls. Most of these skulls are less than ten years old and hardly any are older than twenty years. These skulls are carved mainly in China and Brazil but also in Japan, Germany, Nepal, Mexico and some other countries. There are several crystal skull venders who send raw material to China where they are carved into skulls and sent back to sell. The style varies over time, although during certain periods the style shows strong similarities. Nowadays it is easier to buy contemporary crystal skulls than it was ten years ago.[1]

In general, the crystal skulls carved in Brazil are less detailed than the ones carved in China. Some of the skulls carved in Brazil were initially rather simply, almost primitively carved, especially those carved around twenty years ago in the mid 1980s [see Fig. 27]. Over time they have become very attractive, although some Brazilian carvers delivered high quality from the beginning.

Sometimes carving a crystal skull is an exceptional act for a carver. This may lead to rather unique shapes. Good examples of this are the first two skulls I acquired: Egaddon (white calcite, carved around the end of the 1980s) and Sam (clear quartz, carved in 1996) [see Fig. 28].

Photo © Amayra Hamilton

Fig. 27. Brazilian simple carving from amethyst from the early 1990s.

Contemporary Skulls Have the Same Potential as Old/Ancient Ones

People who work intensely with their contemporary skulls will have many stories to tell. Joshua Shapiro has shared these stories in his e-book.[2] Jeanne and I have had similar experiences with our crystal skulls. We hold weekly crystal skull meditations in our house, and it is remarkable that only rarely will people pick up the two old/ancient skulls or the three fully activated Nepal skulls we have. The contemporary skulls provide them with everything they want to experience.

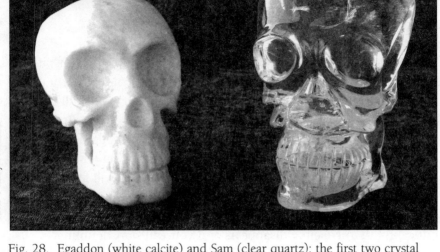

Fig. 28. Egaddon (white calcite) and Sam (clear quartz): the first two crystal skulls collected by the author and his wife Jeanne.

It is my belief that contemporary skulls have the same potential as old and ancient skulls. Most people use only a certain portion of what is available when they work with a crystal skull because they are not yet able to experience the full range of activation of ancient crystal skulls. This means that the contemporary crystal skulls give them everything and every experience their system can handle.

The depth of experiences one can have with contemporary crystal skulls has been described beautifully in *Crystal Skulls: Emissaries of Healing and Sacred Wisdom*, by Marion Webb-De Sisto. This book is solely dedicated to experiences with contemporary crystal skulls. If you have any doubt about the value and importance of contemporary crystal skulls, this book will change your mind. It helps the reader to see the power contemporary crystal skulls can have for healing, spiritual awakening and life-changing encounters. Those experiences are similar to those of Joshua and Desy Shapiro, as well as to those of Jeanne and me.

Finding Your Skull

You may not yet have a crystal skull to work with yet feel inspired to obtain one. Knowing that there are places where you can get a crystal skull, a question may come up: "How do I find a crystal skull that will be good for me? How do I find *my* crystal skull?" Different people may give you different answers to this question, but it boils down to one thing—trust! Trust the signals and feelings you will get when you connect with a crystal skull that resonates with you. You will feel an immediate attraction. When you feel such an attraction, do not hesitate and do not analyze these feelings. As soon as you move to your analyzing critical mind, the feeling disappears and you will start doubting.

Some people have asked whether it is possible to buy the "wrong" contemporary crystal skull. My answer is simply: "I do not think so." It may be possible that you connect with your crystal skull less deeply than you expected. Realize that it is only your expectation and the consequent disappointments that may give you the feeling that you bought the wrong crystal skull. There could be many reasons why you connect less deeply with your crystal skull. It may reflect a general inability to connect deeply. You might be afraid to connect more deeply. Crystal skulls invite us to look beyond and to see every situation as a wonderful opportunity to learn more about ourselves.

In most cases, when people have felt an attraction and decide to purchase a crystal skull, they will usually work with their crystal skull quite a bit. For some people, it is the beginning of an intense journey. For others, they will work with crystal skulls for a period of time. Whatever may be the case, it will always give you what you need in that phase of your life. As we mentioned before: Be careful! Once you truly connect with a crystal skull, you may soon get the feeling that other skulls start "calling" you, and before you realize it, you have a whole family [see Plate 10 and Plate 20].

Some people say that it is not you who selects a crystal skull, but the crystal skull that selects you. I believe both have truth. You feel attracted to a crystal skull because that crystal skull has a vibration that you can easily resonate with, and you recognize that resonance through the feeling you have for that crystal skull. At the same time, your energy awakens the energy of the crystal skull. The crystal skull resonates with aspects of your energy, and it consequently vibrates stronger than any of the other crystal skulls. It is "calling" the person whose energy induces its activation through his or her resonance with that crystal skull.

A subject that has frequently been brought up is the size of a crystal skull: "What size is most optimal for me?" What has been said about finding a crystal skull through feeling a connection is the way to go. Size will be secondary. Nonetheless, I would like to make a few comments on size.

Many people feel that the larger a crystal skull, the better it is. I would like to state clearly that this is not true. For personal use, a small crystal skull is enough and often even better. They are less expensive, less heavy and much easier to meditate with. I have heard people say that a larger crystal skull can contain more information. That is absolutely true. However, a whole library can be stored in a crystal the size of a sugar cube. A crystal skull of two inches in length has the size of several sugar cubes. As individuals, we will never fill the storage space a crystal skull of that size gives us. If you are looking for a crystal skull for personal use, a small crystal skull is large enough. Only when you use crystal skulls for other reasons—for example, for creating special energy fields—you may want to choose larger crystal skulls. We will look at the relationship between crystal skulls and energy fields later in the book.

Connecting with crystal skulls, whether they are contemporary or made a long time ago, is an adventure that is truly life-changing. As we will see in Part 2, these skulls have an effect on our health and well-being, as they are capable of realigning our energy systems, such as the chakras and the meridians. Crystal skulls can reflect to us aspects of ourselves, giving us opportunities to either enjoy these aspects or to change them. Even more importantly, they help us to connect to information that may help us to change how we see the world. People who regularly participate in our weekly crystal skull meditations state that these crystal skulls have truly changed their lives.

PART 2

The Crystal Skull Energies

This section looks at the different types of energy that are connected with crystal skulls. Although some information is scientific, there is also much information that is not based on current scientific paradigms. A discussion about the energies of crystal skulls is essential for a deeper understanding of them. As I said before, it will not be possible to understand crystal skulls based on a scientific approach only. This means that much of the information presented in Part 2 is based on experiences and psychic methods. This requires that readers feel for themselves what they choose to believe or not. It also invites them to actively participate in the journey of discovering the different energies connected with crystal skulls. Hopefully this will lead to more studies on the energies of crystal skulls to allow us a deeper understanding of this phenomenon.

CHAPTER 5

The DiffeRenτ EneRgies Connecτed wiτh CRysτal Skulls

E verything is energy. The world, the whole universe consists of energies vibrating at different frequencies. Thanks to Einstein, we know that even solid matter is energy. Energies can be separated into the energies belonging to what the physicist David Bohm calls the *explicate order*, the world of the visible, and the energies of the world of the invisible, the *implicate order*.[1] The world of the explicate order is the world we know as our physical world. We perceive this world with our physical senses. This is the world that most people believe is all there is.

Many people believe that what we perceive is the complete world, although we are beginning to realize that this perception and belief is an illusion. Our senses only register that aspect of the physical reality which falls within the range of what our senses can perceive—everything outside of that "does not exist." We live in the illusion that what we perceive is all there is.

But reality is more than what our five senses perceive—for example, humans hear a different range of frequencies than, for instance, a dog. Furthermore, how our brain interprets the signals and information is colored by our beliefs. Our belief structures determine the interpretation of reality. For that reason, different people will often describe an event differently. In the interpretation of all the signals that reach their brain, they bring different accents into what actually happened, sometimes leading to dramatic differences in their stories of the event. Understanding that many of the differences that seem to exist are only reflecting peoples' different ways of perceiving the same world can help us to honor these differences and learn from them.

Quantum physics and people like David Bohm help us to see that the only way to truly understand the world we live in is by including the implicate order, the unseen world, the world of subtle energies. It is my belief that we cannot understand crystal skulls without including the subtle energies, the implicate order of the world. Up until now, the world of subtle energies has been mainly the world of psychics and seers. Increasingly, it is also the world of quantum physics.

Understanding the concept of energies is important to understanding ourselves and the way we interact with our environment. Being energy beings, the only true healing comes from energy healing. There is an increasing awareness that the healing of the future will be energy, or vibration, healing.

To understand the phenomenon of crystal skulls, we have to look at their energetic aspects. Research on the energies of crystal skulls is only in its beginning phase. However, it is important to at least summarize the most important aspects of the crystal skull energies. We will look at the following types of energies that are connected to crystal skulls:

* The energies of the electromagnetic field around crystal skulls.
* Piezoelectric energy, which is mostly known in relation to quartz crystal skulls.
* The energy fields around crystal skulls that I call polyhedral fields.
* The energy (frequencies) of crystal skulls that makes them resonate with the original thirteen skulls. (These energies will be the subject of Part 3 of this book.)

We will also look at how we can interact with these different crystal skull energies and what their effects are on human beings.

CRysTals as Tools FoR Healing

We know that every physical object, whether it is "alive" according to biological terms or not, has an electromagnetic field. It may be weak, but as long as electrons move, there is a current and consequently electricity, and thus also a magnetic field. Every type of energy will resonate with similar energies or the overtones of these energies. We, as human beings, have electromagnetic fields that relate to all levels of activity within our system.

Part of balancing the functions of the activities in our physical system is through energy medicine, or vibrational healing. Many people believe that when one or more of their systems are out of balance, crystals and crystal skulls can provide an energy field that contributes to the balancing of these systems. When people use crystals and crystal skulls as tools for healing, they rarely specify the type of energies they work with. Another issue is that there is hardly any scientific research done that demonstrates that crystals and crystals skulls do indeed have an effect on the human energy system.

There are an increasing number of signs indicating that energy healing may be the answer to many problems our current medical institutions are unable to resolve. The disadvantages of chemical treatments are more than apparent and alternatives are needed. It would be wonderful if crystals and crystal skulls would be included as tools in energy healing. At the moment, the regular medical world is still skeptical, although we see that some energy healing modalities are entering some institutions. It is likely that crystals and crystal skulls will play their role in the future of energy medicine.

Science tends to believe that the effects people experience with crystals and crystal skulls are due to a placebo effect. This is one way of perceiving positive effects. However, any positive change is a change for the better and will make it easier to continue to create more changes. Fundamentally, it does not make a difference what causes a positive change. What does make a difference is whether the change leads to a change in beliefs, because only then can the change become permanent instead of temporary.

Based on my observations, I believe that crystals and crystal skulls have many positive effects on people. However, there are claims about the healing powers of crystals that in my opinion border on irresponsibility. Illnesses are not cured by putting a crystal or crystal skull in your pocket. It is more complicated and more subtle than that. The fact that different people in the crystal field describe different effects from the same type of crystal is for me an indication that we have to be very careful with what we say.

Often we do not (yet) fully understand all the energetic effects of crystals and crystal skulls on our complex human energy system. Crystal skulls and crystals can support us in many ways, but they never take over our responsibilities. They are a divine gift, and no divine gift will ever take away our free will. So I urgently request the reader to never give your power away to any tool, as wonderful as that tool may be. You always remain responsible for every choice, every belief you have and every creation in your life.

The Electromagnetic Field Around Crystal Skulls

As far as I know, there are no published studies of the electromagnetic fields of crystal skulls. I did some preliminary studies that, although they've so far been done on a small scale, are worthwhile to share. The method I used in these studies was Resonance Field Imaging™.[2]

Resonance Field Imaging™ (RFI™) is a method to help us understand the energies around human beings, plants, animals and objects. It can also measure *ambient energy*, the energy of the surroundings. RFI™ is defined as an experimental electromagnetic feedback and imaging process. It gives detailed scientific information and objective interpretations for all auras and bioenergy fields. It even identifies the type and function of all bioenergies present in specific regions of the human brain. RFI™ is a method or process that requires copyrighted materials and is driven by an intricate system of calculations and formulas.[3] It is based on the principle that every living and nonliving object has an electromagnetic field around it.

To measure electromagnetic energies, a counter is used that measures these frequencies in the range from 1 MHz to 3 GHz. Different frequency ranges are connected to one of fifteen basic colors, which describe the quality of the energies. Based on data collected over many years, a computer program has been developed to analyze the frequencies that are measured around a human being. This will give information about the physical condition, the psychological condition and the condition of the chakras of the measured person.

I selected this system to help me to understand more of the electro-magnetic energy system of crystal skulls. I started the measurements of our crystal skulls on the deck of our house in Clarkdale, Arizona, in front of the window of the room in which our large collection of skulls (over 130) were standing in a circle. Each crystal skull tested was placed on a table facing away from the house. This meant that the back of the skull was facing toward the house. The frequencies were measured at four distances on five sides of the skull: the right side, the left side, in front, in back and above the skull. The distances were two inches, four inches, eight inches and twelve inches. The measured frequencies at the four distances were averaged for each of the five sides of the skull. These averages form the data I have worked with to indicate the main frequencies we experience with that crystal skull in that place in that position. I used this method to measure twenty-three crystal skulls of different sizes and materials.

I organized the measured crystal skulls into three groups. The first group was formed by quartz crystal skulls with a size close to six inches and larger (up to eight inches for a dark amethyst skull). In this group were clear quartz, smoky quartz, citrine, rose quartz and amethyst. The second group was formed by crystal skulls carved from quartz with a size from three to four inches. The third group was formed by skulls that were made of material other than quartz and their size was around six inches. The results are summarized in Table 1. In this table, I have given the total range of the frequencies in megahertz measured at each of the five sides. For the three groups, I have also given the range of frequencies as the percentage of the total range of frequencies of all skulls studied ("Total" in the table).

AT OUR HOUSE (CLARKDALE, ARIZONA)		Total (23 Skulls)	Large Quartz (8 Skulls)	Small Quartz (8 Skulls)	Large Non-Quartz (7 Skulls)
RIGHT	Range	526.4–578.7	526.4–568.8	559.1–569.0	548.6–578.7
	Percentage		81.1%	18.9%	57.6%
LEFT	Range	543.6–563.7	548.5–562.4	543.6–550.9	554.7–563.7
	Percentage		70.2%	36.7%	45.5%
FRONT	Range	259.3–367.9	259.3–346.9	325.8–367.9	277.1–336.1
	Percentage	•	80.7%	38.8%	59.0%
BACK	Range	362.1–467.6	362.1–437.7	419.8–467.6	425.0–449.9
	Percentage		75.6%	47.8%	51.7%
ABOVE	Range	177.9–289.4	177.9–289.4	219.6–237.5	190.7–230.3
	Percentage		100%	17.8%	35.5%

Table 1. Measured frequencies in megahertz at five places around crystal skulls, which are organized in three groups: eight large quartz crystal skulls (six to eight inches), eight small crystal skulls (three to four inches) and seven large crystal skulls carved out of materials other than quartz (around six inches). Measurements have been given as the total range of frequencies measured for all skulls and for each of the three groups. For the three groups, the range of frequencies is also given as a percentage of the total range of all measured skulls.

The results indicate that all crystal skulls show the same basic pattern. There are rather high frequencies at the right and the left side, lower frequencies in the front and in the back, and the lowest frequencies above the skulls. When we look at the range of the measured frequencies, those at the left side are smaller than those of the other four sides. The range of frequencies (frequency band) on the left side falls completely within the range of the frequencies on the right side. In the group of the smaller quartz crystal skulls and the non-quartz crystal skulls, the measured range of frequencies of the front, back and above have no overlap at all. With the large quartz skulls, there are small overlaps. The range of frequencies of the small quartz skulls is the smallest, the range of frequencies of the large quartz skulls is the largest and the range of frequencies of the crystal skulls made of other materials is in between. The smaller quartz skulls, independent of the type of quartz they are made from, have a rather narrow range of frequencies which may indicate that they are more specific or maybe more restricted in their function than the larger quartz skulls. The crystal skulls made from other materials than quartz also seem to be more specific than the large quartz crystal skulls.

When a crystal skulls was measured a couple of times within a period of one to two weeks, most of the variation between these measurements was found in the front, the back and above, hardly in the right and left sides. I realized that the energy field of the crystal skulls in the room behind the crystal skull that I measured had a strong influence on the energy at the back, front and top. This energy field may have influenced the measurements. I suspected that the measured crystal skulls were interacting with the energy field created by the skulls in the room behind them. Each crystal skull was interacting with this field of the group of skulls in the room in a slightly different way. Consequently, the measurements in the back, front and above had a wider variation than the measurements at the right and left sides.

The results that I describe above were in the first instance disappointing. I expected large differences between the different skulls. However, that was not what I found. Actually, the similarity between the different skulls was rather striking. I had to measure quite a number of crystal skulls before I began to see a pattern.

These results brought up a question: What would the frequencies be if the measurements were done at other locations? So I selected a few other places to compare the frequencies with the ones I measured on the balcony of our house in Clarkdale. I selected two other places: one was on a picnic table in Dead Horse Ranch State Park in Cottonwood, Arizona (about a mile from our house as the crow flies), and the other was inside a building in a session room at Angel Valley Spiritual Retreat Center in Sedona (sixteen miles from our house). I also took Sam (our large clear quartz crystal skull) to two additional places, both located in the red rock area of Sedona: one near Devil's Bridge and the other one on top of a small hill in front of Chimney Rock. Table 2 summarizes the results:

LOCATION					
	Near Our House in Clarkdale, Arizona (23 Skulls)	Dead Horse Ranch State Park in Cottonwood, Arizona (4 Skulls)	Angel Valley Spiritual Retreat Center in Sedona, Arizona (6 Skulls)	Devil's Bridge in Sedona, Arizona (1 Skull)	Small Hill in Front of Chimney Rock in Sedona, Arizona (1 Skull)
RIGHT	626.4–578.7	532.4–550.9	385.5–407.3	319.8	250.1
Size Range	52.3	18.5	21.8	N/A	N/A
LEFT	543.6–563.4	518.3–567.0	296.9–359.5	296.4	220.0
Size Range	19.8	48.7	62.6	N/A	N/A
FRONT	259.3–367.9	497.9–517.6	187.2–220.8	240.2	277.6
Size Range	108.6	19.7	33.6	N/A	N/A
BACK	362.1–467.6	541.6–562.5	212.8–336.5	304.1	159.9
Size Range	105.5	20.9	123.7	N/A	N/A
ABOVE	177.9–289.4	534.4–571.1	185.8–189.5	243.1	214.4
Size Range	111.5	37.2	3.7	N/A	N/A

Table 2. Comparison of frequencies and frequency ranges indicated in megahertz of five places around crystal skulls in five different locations in Arizona.

The results show some interesting patterns. In the first place, it becomes clear that the difference between locations is larger than the variation within a location. The results are remarkable at the Dead Horse Ranch State Park in the second column. Here the five places measured around the crystal skulls did not show as much variation as in other locations. In that particular situation, there was no specific energy source in the area influencing the measurement. This was not the case in the session room at Angel Valley. In this room, there are all kinds of objects that create energy fields, similar to the situation at the balcony of our house where we have the energy field induced by the crystal skulls in the room behind the measured crystal skull.

In general, it seems that the measurements taken in a natural environment (Dead Horse Ranch State Park and the two locations in Sedona) show less variation between the five places around a crystal skull than in the measurements done inside or close to a house. This does not mean that results within one place do not differ; we saw that already with the results presented in Table 1. This is confirmed when we look at the clear quartz crystal skull Sam measured at different times [see Table 3].

LOCATION				
	Our House 6/6/06	Our House 6/27/06	Our House 6/27/06	Our House 6/29/06
RIGHT	539.9	565.3	565.8	554.0
LEFT	563.1	551.3	549.6	552.9
FRONT	357.6	229.9	284.6	282.3
BACK	336.2	362.1	400.0	379.3
ABOVE	270.1	289.4	223.9	262.5

Table 3. Measurements of the clear quartz crystal skull Sam at different times in the same position at the same place (on the balcony of our house in Clarkdale, Arizona).

The results show that there is variation in frequencies at the same location at different moments. However, this variation does not change the overall pattern. The differences are also much smaller than the differences between locations.

Another interesting aspect is the degree of variation between the different sides of the skulls. In Table 2 we see that near our house the larger variations are found in front, back and above the skull. At Dead Horse Ranch State Park, the largest variation was found at the left side, whereas the variation at the left side was still rather small on the balcony at our house. At Angel Valley in the session room, the largest variation was found at the back and also at the left. I mentioned already that these variations could be induced by an energy source that comes from a certain direction, like the circle of crystal skulls in our house. At Angel Valley, it was most likely the collection of essential oils and certain crystals in the room. To test this idea, Sam was measured in three different positions at the same location, again at our house in Clarkdale. The standard position we had been using was the skull facing south, away from the house. The skull was turned 90 degrees facing east and then 180 degrees facing north (toward the house). The following results were obtained [see Table 4].

POSITION			
	Standard (Facing South)	**Turned 90°** (Facing East)	**Turned 180°** (Facing North)
RIGHT	565.8	385.6	546.8
LEFT	551.3	354.1	578.1
FRONT	299.9	514.4	387.2
BACK	362.1	530.7	309.2
ABOVE	289.4	507.3	356.4

Table 4. Measurements of the electromagnetic energies in the megahertz range around the crystal skull Sam on the balcony of our house in Clarkdale, Arizona, with Sam placed with its face turned toward different directions.

The results confirm the idea that energy fields may influence the measured frequencies. There is a similar pattern with the skull in the standard position (facing south) and when the skull is turned 180 degrees. In both cases, the right and left sides have the highest frequencies, and those frequencies are in the same range. However, when the skull is turned 90 degrees, the results are different. Now the frequencies of the front and back look more like the frequencies of the left and right side of the previous positions, whereas the frequencies of the left and right go more in the direction of the frequencies of the front and back. The frequencies measured above seem to be more determined by what happens at the front and back than by what happens at the right and left side. The results presented in Table 4 seem to confirm the idea that a source of energy influences the measurements around a crystal skull. To what degree different types of crystal skulls influence the energies induced by the environment and what the determining factors for these influences may be is at the moment still unclear.

Summarizing, we can draw a few conclusions. When we measure the electromagnetic frequencies in the megahertz range around crystal skulls, it becomes clear that although there are differences between skulls, these differences are not very large. These small differences seem to be influenced by size and by the material the crystal skull is carved from. The differences in frequencies between crystal skulls measured in one location are surely smaller than the differences in frequencies found between different locations. When we look at the differences between crystal skulls, we notice that the differences are the largest between large quartz skulls (skulls of six to eight inches), less between smaller quartz skulls (three to four inches), and in between those two groups for large crystals skulls made from material other than quartz.

Earlier I mentioned that crystal skulls are reflectors. The measurement of the electromagnetic energies around crystal skulls seems to indicate that the measured frequencies reflect the environment more than the energies of the crystal skull itself. In that sense, crystal skulls are truly reflectors of their environment. It is only a small step from here to believe that when we hold a crystal skull, we are the environment—or at least the most determining energy factor in the environment—and consequently the crystal skull will reflect us to ourselves.

Piezoelectricity and Crystals

To understand some of the characteristics of crystal skulls, it is important to include a phenomenon called piezoelectricity. Although piezoelectricity is mainly used in technology, it is also used, often unconsciously, when we work with crystal skulls. Let us first look at what piezoelectricity is.

Piezoelectricity was discovered by Pierre Curie in 1883, and its name is derived from the Greek word *piezin*, which means to squeeze or press. When mechanical stress is applied to a crystal, it produces a voltage across the material. So a piezoelectric crystal can produce an electrical field. In reverse, an electrical field creates a mechanical deformation in crystals. This means that especially quartz crystals provide a convenient transducer effect between electrical and mechanical oscillations.

For this reason, piezoelectricity is applied in many technologies. In many of these technological devices, quartz has been used. Nowadays, many ceramic materials that exhibit piezoelectric qualities have been developed. The technologies in which piezoelectricity is used include sonar, watches, radio, television and many more. Quartz crystals are also used in the transducer probes of ultrasound machines.

Not all crystals and thus crystal skulls exhibit piezoelectricity. Only those crystals that do not have a center of symmetry exhibit it. Most people believe that it is only quartz that exhibits piezoelectric qualities, but that is not true. There are twenty-one crystal classes that exhibit piezoelectricity. The term "crystal class" comes from the discipline of crystallography, which has developed a descriptive terminology that is applied to crystals and crystal features in order to describe their structure, symmetry and shape.

This terminology defines the crystal lattice, which provides a mineral with its ordered internal structure, and it also describes various types of symmetry. By considering what type of symmetry a mineral species possesses, the species may be categorized as a member of one of six crystal systems and one of thirty-two crystal classes. Of all crystals that exhibit piezoelectricity, quartz and Rochelle salt exhibit the strongest. Piezoelectricity is also found in many crystals that are part of our human system. Bone has piezoelectric characteristics—at least dry bone. Whether bone in life circumstances shows the same characteristics is still a debate.

In general, it is believed that many different electromagnetic frequencies will induce a piezoelectric effect in crystals. This means that even our thoughts can create this phenomenon, because our thoughts have an electromagnetic frequency. Several of the characteristics described for crystal skulls and crystals are based on piezoelectric qualities. For example, there is a belief that when you meditate with a crystal skull and send out a certain intention, it will help you because the crystal skull will strengthen that intention. But the intention has a certain electromagnetic frequency that will "de-form" the crystal. This means that it will then send out again the same frequencies to you, helping you to intensify your intent.

This will be true for all crystal skulls that are made from material that has piezoelectric qualities. This means they will be the strongest for crystal skulls made from quartz. Realize that this principle is different from programming a crystal skull, as we mentioned in Part 1. That is based on the ability of crystal skulls to store information.

Activation and Polyhedral Fields

An important part of the work with crystals and crystal skulls involves activation. You hear people say they have fully activated their crystal skull or crystal. In the initial period, when I was becoming more acquainted with crystal skulls and crystals, I was always puzzled by what exactly they mean by "fully activated." As I perceived it, the crystals or crystal skulls that people called fully activated had different levels of energy. However, at that time I had no way to understand the differences I perceived.

Many years back, during a healing session, I perceived certain instabilities in the aura of a person that seemed to be different from anything I had experienced so far. I had no idea what it meant, let alone how to work with it, so I asked my guides for help. In those days, my attempts to connect with my guides did not always result in a clear answer or understanding; sometimes it led to even more confusion. However, this was one of the times that I did receive a clear answer.

My guides showed me that besides the energy bodies that exist around the physical body, there are frequency bands around a human being. There are many of those frequency bands (more than a hundred) and consequently they are not easily perceived. They also showed me that these fields have a geometric structure, consisting of sometimes irregularly shaped triangles, squares and pentagons of various sizes. There are many of these geometric forms in a field—these are called polyhedral fields. They told me that if any of these fields is out of balance, it will create imbalance in a person, be it on an emotional or mental level. I was challenged to see and describe something I had not heard about before, so I asked several psychics. They could feel the truth, even sense the presence of these polyhedral fields, but like me, they had difficulty seeing all the details.

One day, while I was meditating on the subject of the activation of crystal skulls, the memory of polyhedral fields being shown to me suddenly came back. A rush of energy told me I was on the right track. Since then, a lot of time and energy has been spent on understanding the phenomenon of polyhedral fields (PHFs) in relation to crystal skulls and crystals. Although the system of PHFs is something not everybody may be able to relate to, it has significantly helped me to understand activation, the differences between crystals and crystal skulls, the differences between contemporary and ancient crystal skulls, and the interac-

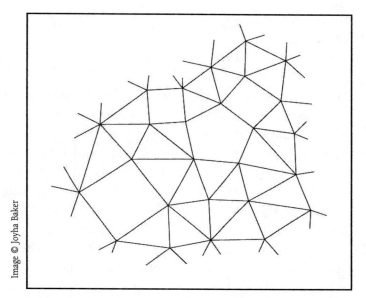

Image © Joyha Baker

Fig. 29. A part of a polyhedral field (PHF) to show the variation in the size and the shape of the faces that form the PHF.

tion of our consciousness with crystal skulls. Sharing about PHFs may lead to a deeper understanding of activation and the energy systems of crystal skulls in general.

In Fig. 29, part of a polyhedral field has been drawn. A PHF is not a static field but a dynamic one. It resonates within a certain frequency range, and because of this dynamic characteristic, the qualities and colors change constantly. In a human being, there are so many PHFs that so far I have not been able to distinguish the many layers. With crystal skulls and crystals, the situation is simpler. Over time I discovered that there is a maximum of only twelve PHFs connected with crystal skulls and crystals.

Although distinguishing between the separate PHFs of crystal skulls is easier than with human beings, the activated PHFs form a dynamic whole and the frequencies and colors depend on our interactions with them.

When you pick up a crystal skull or crystal, there is an immediate change in it due to your interaction. When you focus on a crystal skull or crystal, the energy changes even more. This means that it requires training and perseverance to study the PHFs of crystal skulls.

In the initial phase, I was mainly focused on the question of how many PHFs a particular crystal skull or crystal has. In those days, our crystal skulls were not yet very active, so I discovered that crystal skulls hardly ever have more than nine PHFs. I never found a crystal skull larger than about two inches that had less than six PHFs. I also found that crystals that had never been worked with or worked with only minimally had a lower number of PHFs than crystal skulls, but the number was never below four PHFs. It seemed that the basic number of PHFs of crystal skulls was higher than that of crystals. The smaller crystal skulls (less than two inches) formed an exception—most of them only had four PHFs. I used to joke that they looked like crystal skulls, but they were not—at least not when you looked at them from an energetic point of view. Later we learned that through activation they could still make the "jump" to crystal skulls. Let me explain what this jump is.

One day I had the opportunity to look at the number of PHFs of a crystal before it was carved. I followed the process until the skull was finished [see Plates 12–15]. This confirmed what earlier observations suggested: When a crystal is carved into a crystal skull, the number of PHFs increases from four to at least six or from five to at least seven. This change induces a shift in the energies that moves the new skull from the collective crystal energy field into the collective crystal skull energy field.

Most people are familiar with the collective unconsciousness. This is a term first used by the German psychiatrist Carl Gustav Jung. However, there are many collective fields. Every animal has a collective field. Humans know many collective fields. One of the smaller collective fields is that of a family. Another small collective field that is temporary is the collective field created during a workshop. The only way to create a col-

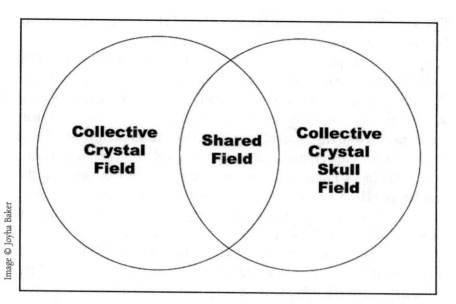

Fig. 30. A symbolic representation of the collective crystal field, the collective crystal skull field and the area of energies they share together.

lective field is when there are energies that are similar and that are shared in one way or another. In this way, crystals form a field (with subfields like clear quartz and lapis lazuli) and crystal skulls form a field. The collective crystal field and the collective crystal skull field share a part of their fields. This part is represented by the energies of the first four PHFs and some of the fifth PHF [see Fig. 30]. The collective crystal skull field has several subfields, which we'll look at later.

Once Jeanne and I understood the principle of the PHFs as a system of measuring the level of activation, a new phase in our work with crystal skulls began. Before I describe that phase, I would like to answer a question people regularly ask me: "How do you know how many PHFs a crystal skull or crystal has?" It is not easy to answer this question, in the same way as it is not easy to answer how I know the condition of somebody's chakras. As with chakras, the first step is the acceptance that something exists. If you do not believe PHFs exist, you will never be able to feel them or sense them or dowse them.

For some people, the easiest way to define the number of PHFs and/or the number of sublevels is by dowsing them. The other way is to develop your sensitivity so you can literally see them or feel them or simply know how many there are. As with everything in life, it is a matter of training—in this case, of your intuition and sensitivity. My way is to connect with the crystal skull or crystal. I feel the vibration, and due to my training, I immediately recognize the level of vibration and the number of PHFs that are connected to that level. It has become almost as easy as looking at a flower and knowing the color or as looking at a chakra and knowing the main aspects of its condition.

For a long time, our focus was on raising the number of PHFs. Soon it became clear that a crystal skull did not immediately move from one PHF to the next, despite our intent and attempts to activate it. Two things were discovered: In the first place, the level of activation depended more on us than on the crystal skull. We needed to be ready before we could move the number of PHFs to a higher level. Secondly, we discovered that each PHF has sublevels, or frequency bands. The number of these sublevels was again twelve. This means that there are in total 144 (12 x 12) levels of vibration belonging to a crystal skull and to a crystal. I have never seen a crystal lower than PHF 4 sublevel 3, and I have never seen a crystal skull lower than PHF 6 sublevel 3.

Working with the different PHFs and their sublevels helped us to understand activation. It became clear that Jeanne and I could increase the number of PHFs through intent. However, we could not activate all PHFs and their sublevels at once. We could not go beyond the number of PHFs and their vibration that our consciousness at that moment could connect with. Regularly meditating with the crystal skulls and each time connecting with the highest level of activation slowly increased the number of PHFs and at the same time expanded our consciousness.

I call the activation that leads to an increase in number of PHFs or their sublevels *vertical activation*. Within each sublevel, there is an activation of all the potential of that sublevel. This kind of activation I called *horizontal activation*. It is possible to use vertical activation even when the horizontal activation is not completed. However, a certain amount of horizontal activation is needed before the next step in vertical activation. Otherwise, the vertical activation becomes very difficult, if not impossible.

For the next couple of years, we activated our crystal skulls step by step to higher levels. Our activation was based on intent. Our intent was to activate a crystal skull to the next sublevel, and we did that as often as we needed to allow our consciousness to expand enough to induce the activation to that next level. As the number of PHFs increased, the size of the energy field they created also increased.

The activation worked all the way until we had activated a number of our contemporary crystal skulls to PHF 12 sublevel 3. Then I got stuck. Whatever my intent was, there was no longer an increase in the frequencies of the sublevels. It took awhile before I found out what was going on. To understand what happened, we needed to look first at the ancient crystal skulls.

Initially, I thought that ancient crystal skulls were also not completely activated. Whenever I worked with an ancient crystal skull, I could experience only a certain number of the PHFs. It took me a long time to realize that this had nothing to do with the level of activation of the skull but with my state of awareness. I could not experience, sense and see those higher levels, because I was not yet able to connect with them. For that reason, it took me many years before I realized that ancient and old skulls (at least the ones I am familiar with) are actually activated on all 144 levels. I realized this the moment I made a deep connection with our small fully activated crystal skull Ti [see Plate 8]. I will never forget the experience of intense happiness that came with this connection. Let me share how that happened.

I mentioned earlier that we are the caretakers of two small fully activated crystal skulls, Ti and Bet. For me, Ti is the easier one to connect with. One day I was meditating with Ti, and instead of focusing on the crystal skull and trying to read and understand the energies (which is an active meditation and a masculine approach), I moved into a state of relaxation and I felt my heart open. The best way to describe it is that I suddenly felt a deep love for this skull. It felt that the boundaries between me and the crystal skull fell away, and we merged. I felt a change in myself and experienced a deep joy.

I knew I had made a full connection with Ti, experiencing all twelve PHFs and all 144 frequencies in their fullness. Being in that state, I suddenly knew: the last steps toward a complete activation are not done through intent but simply by becoming one with the crystal skull through a connection with the heart. It is not through action but through being (a feminine approach) that this full connection can be made. Once again, I was reminded that a state of being is more powerful than a state of action or directing. Being in that state, I also knew that all ancient and old crystal skulls are fully activated. I can feel the complete activation only when I connect with a crystal skull through my heart.

Using my experience and connection with Ti as my point of reference, I was able to activate all twelve sublevels of the twelfth PHF of some of our other crystal skulls. It still required focus and a deep connection with the heart, but it was no longer out of reach. Once we had some of the crystal skulls activated over all 144 frequencies, we still had to focus on horizontal activation. The first of our skulls that became fully activated was Sam, the human-sized clear quartz crystal skull. At the time this book was completed, about 20 percent of our crystal skulls were fully activated. The other crystal skulls are at different levels in the process of activating all frequency levels both vertically and horizontally. I have noticed that it is easier for me to activate all levels of quartz crystal skulls than of those made of other materials. It makes me realize that there is still much to discover.

The fact that I am able to activate all 144 frequencies does not mean at this point in time that I know how to access the information stored in the crystal skulls. As was mentioned in Part 1, that requires an understanding of the way the information was programmed, which is quite a different matter.

Later in my studies of PHFs, I discovered a phenomenon that has helped me to better understand the differences between crystal skulls and crystals. The increase in the number of PHFs when a crystal is carved into a crystal skull cannot truly explain the energetic differences between crystals and crystal skulls that many people experience. A crystal can also be activated and get to twelve PHFs with twelve sub-levels in each PHF. One would assume this would make a crystal more or less similar to a crystal skull; however, that is not what Jeanne and I and other people have experienced. In general, I am not very visual in my meditations, but sometimes clear images come up or are shown. One day, when I was in meditation, again pondering about the differences between crystal skulls and crystals, I suddenly saw images that made it all clear and very simple to me. I had been able to feel that when a crystal is carved into a crystal skull, something shifts. Up until that moment, I believed that the only thing that changed was the number of PHFs. However, I found that it is more than that—also, the quality and frequency of the PHFs that are connected to crystal skulls are different when compared to those of crystals.

Let me give an example and start with a crystal with four PHFs. If I activate this crystal as a crystal, the fifth and the sixth PHF will have a certain frequency range. However, when that same crystal is carved into a crystal skull, the frequency band of the fifth and sixth PHF will be even higher. The frequency band of the fifth PHF of the crystal skull will be in between the frequency ranges of the fifth and sixth of the crystal. This is true for all crystal skull PHFs—they are all higher in frequency than the same PHF of an activated crystal. Crystal skulls literally shift into a different state of being and energy field: the collective crystal skull field. As I explained earlier, this field is different from the collective crystal field, although these two fields share a common basis in the first four PHFs.

It may be helpful to give an image of the different PHFs around a crystal skull [see Fig. 31]. The lines show the center of each of the twelve PHFs. In the image, I have not indicated the width of each PHF, because

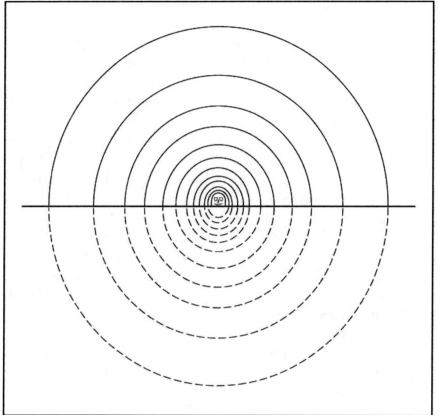

Fig. 31. The twelve polyhedral fields around a crystal skull. Due to the interference of the surface the crystal skull stands on, the lower half of the field will usually be deformed. Shown here are the centers of each of the PHFs. The distance is the average of eight measurements.

during the interaction with the crystal skull, the width of a PHF changes continuously. When the number of PHFs increases, the distance between the PHFs increases as well. Although the distance between the PHFs varies between the different crystal skulls, this difference is small. In Fig. 31, the average of eight crystal skulls is given. The distance from the edge of the crystal skull to the center of the twelfth PHF is on the average 171 cm (5 feet 8 inches).

The Six Additional PHFs

At this point in time, I believed I had discovered all there was about PHFs. However, I soon discovered that there was yet another aspect. This revealed itself when Jeanne and I bought a six-inch nebula stone crystal skull [see Plate 16]. Nebula stone has had my deep interest from the moment I first connected with it in 1999. From the very beginning, the energies connected with nebula stone were different from what I was familiar with when connecting with crystals and crystal skulls, yet it was not easy to define in what way it was different. I jokingly called it "from outer space."

Nebula stone is a rare stone that is found only in the Sierras Madres in Mexico. It was discovered by Ron and Karen Nurnberg, and the exact location is known only to them. Research on the chemical composition has revealed that it is a new stone. So far it has not been scientifically described, because Ron and Karen have not revealed the exact location, which is required for a scientific publication.[4]

I had looked at the number of PHF of two small nebula stone crystal skulls we have in the initial phase of my research, when I was not yet very experienced in establishing the number of PHFs. I use both scanning and sensing to define the different energies and, in this particular case, the PHFs. Scanning is the method I use to get a better feel for what type of energy I am dealing with. It feels like an built-in measuring device that enables me to define the energies in a more detailed way. This method was shown to me during a meditation and I have fine-tuned it over time. It looks like the screen of an inner monitor. Sensing is using senses other than the five normal senses to obtain information about the quality of energies. In general, this is called using psychic abilities.

The new large nebula stone skull invited me to study the PHFs of this stone again. It turned out to be a challenging process. The nebula stone skull definitely has the twelve PHFs in common with all crystal skulls, but there was something more. There was an additional energy, a vibration I had not perceived before. It was obvious that my system was not yet used to connecting with this energy. It was so intriguing that I could not let go until I had defined these "new" energies. The final result was quite amazing. The large nebula stone has the twelve PHFs plus an additional six. The frequency of these additional six PHFs is much higher than the other twelve. Consequently, because I had not expected any additional PHFs, I did not perceive them.

Needless to say, I was curious whether I could find other crystal skulls and crystals that had these additional six PHFs. It turned out that the extra six PHFs was a very rare phenomenon. None of our crystal skulls and crystals had those additional six, with exception of one type of stone (kambaba jasper, also called kabamba jasper, which comes from Madagascar) and a sphere of unknown origin. Some people call kambaba jasper, nebula stone, which is technically not allowed because nebula stone as such is trademarked. Initial unofficial research indicates that nebula stone and kambaba jasper have a similar composition, although the ratio of the components seems to be different. They seem to be the only two stones with a defined name and place of origin that have the same energetic characteristics that are expressed as six extra PHFs.

The riddle is a two-inch sphere that I bought in 1999 on eBay in England. It was advertised as a nebula stone sphere, but as soon as I received the sphere, I knew it was not the nebula stone from Mexico, which was later confirmed by Ron Nurnberg. The person who sold me the sphere did not know where the material came from and also did not want to share with me where she got the sphere. The sphere has strong similarities with kambaba jasper, but there are enough differences to believe that it could be a different stone. Its energies feel different, but both nebula stone and kambaba jasper are quite variable in themselves. Interestingly, this sphere has the same energetic characteristics as nebula stone and kambaba jasper: it has six extra PHFs.

One day I was meditating with a photo of the Mitchell-Hedges crystal skull and with an essence somebody had made from that skull. In that meditation, I went very deep, feeling and exploring the energies of the Mitchell-Hedges Skull. This crystal skull has always felt to me to be different from the other ancient skulls I am familiar with. In that meditation, I suddenly knew what this difference was; I had studied it intensely. Along with the nebula stone skull and stones, and the kambaba jasper, the Mitchell-Hedges Skull also has the six additional PHFs! What makes this crystal skull different from the other ancient crystal skulls? Could it be that this is a characteristic of the singing crystal skulls I mentioned earlier? I am afraid we will have to wait until more singing crystal skulls surface. Only then can we find out whether that is the case. Meanwhile, my search for other crystal skulls or crystals with the extra six PHFs continues.

Although the Mitchell-Hedges crystal skull shares the additional six PHFs with nebula stone and kambaba jasper, there is an important difference: The six additional PHFs of the Mitchell-Hedges crystal skull are all fully activated, which is not the case with those of crystal skulls made out of nebula stone and kambaba jasper. These skulls give us the opportunity to train our system to be able to activate this system of the additional six PHFs. I am convinced that this will give us the experiences we need to more fully understand the Mitchell-Hedges Skull.

The phenomenon of the six additional PHFs easily leads to hypotheses. I'd like to explore one of them: Given the high frequencies of these PHFs, it may be possible that these extra six PHFs have been induced by a consciousness and/or knowledge that is beyond what we currently grasp. Later we will look at this idea in more detail.

Crystal Skulls and Subtle Energies

Subtle energies belong to what David Bohm calls the implicate order. Most energies that cannot be measured directly with current technology are called subtle energies. Although these energies are not yet measurable, there is an increasing amount of data that confirms their existence. The term "subtle energies" is also used to indicate several energies that alternative healing works with, such as meridians, chakras and subtle energy bodies. There are also subtle energies connected with the Earth in the form of energy lines, grids and vortexes (places where energy moves in and/or out of the Earth, or of grid systems connected with the Earth).

We have already discussed one form of subtle energies connected with the crystal skulls: the energies connected with polyhedral fields. For those working with crystal skulls, there is no doubt that there are more types of subtle energies also connected with the skulls. An example is the subtle energies of crystal skulls that lead to healing. Another example is the subtle energies that are transmitted through certain crystal skulls. Also, the larger energy fields created by crystal skulls are fields of subtle energies.

Since these energies are not directly measurable, there is not much information available about this subject. There are many personal stories that may indicate the presence of subtle energies, but the descriptions are often such that explanations other than the presence of subtle energies are possible as well. Due to an increase in the interest in crystal skulls, I expect that more information may become available in the future.

CHAPTER 6

Working with Crystal Skulls

e may not yet understand all the different subtle energies connected with crystal skulls, but we cannot deny one thing: Crystal skulls have an effect on the subtle energy systems of both the Earth and human beings. We will now look at these effects.

Crystal Skulls and Earth Energies

A large part of my personal research and work has been focused on the study of different types of Earth energies. During my research, I felt guided to use crystal skulls to activate different types of energy lines and vortexes. In my opinion, the energies in the lines and vortexes I studied were not optimal, and I wanted to see what would happen if I activated an Earth energy line or vortex with a crystal skull.

The results were more than rewarding. As soon as I activated any type of line or vortex, there was a strong increase in the size of the lines and vortexes. Initially this was only used to see whether there was any effect at all, but later I developed a more systematic research method, measuring the effects of activation with my crystal skull Sam on a certain type of lines, which I defined through dowsing. These lines were very recognizable, because they contained clearly defined sublines. These sublines are

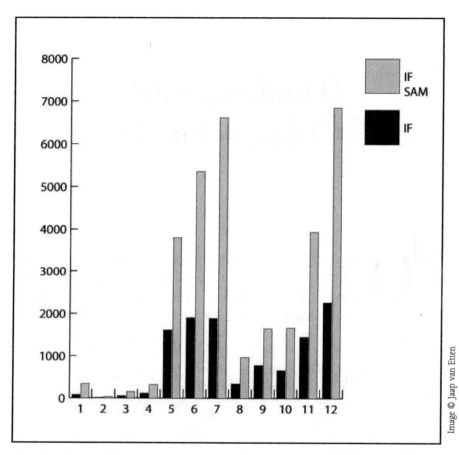

Fig. 32. This graph illustrates the size of the energy lines of the twelve human consciousness grids that are connected with the Earth, indicated as intensity factor (IF), which is calculated by multiplying the height and width of the line, both under natural conditions and after activation with Sam.

called *triads*, because they always contain within themselves three small lines. Because of the presence of triads, it was easy to discover that there were lines with up to twelve of these triads.

The system is rather complex, and this is not the place to go too deep into the characteristics of these lines. However, activating these lines with Sam gave a very clear increase with all twelve different triad lines [see Fig. 32]. I used the term IF (intensity factor) for comparison of the lines. This factor was calculated by multiplying the height of a line with the width of that line. This increase in size was local but immediate and quite explosive. Within a couple of minutes, the energy began to spread through the lines and the local effect began to dissipate. I called this type of activation a direct activation.

I also looked at the phenomenon of indirect activation of Earth energies. Every week we have a crystal skull meditation in our house. One day I decided to measure the size of two vortexes that were located close to our house. One vortex has an energy that resonates with our second chakra and is located about sixty yards away from our crystal skull circle. The second one is a vortex of the triad type I just mentioned, which has twelve triads and is located about forty yards away. I monitored the size of the two vortexes over a couple of weeks, and the results are summarized in Fig. 33.

After every crystal skull meditation, the size of the vortexes increased. Realize that this was not the intent of any of the participants of the meditation. Initially, the participants were not even aware I was taking these measurements. After the increase, there was a slow decrease throughout the week until the next meditation increased the size of both vortexes again.

There is no doubt that meditations with crystal skulls generate an energy field that has a positive and expanding effect on Earth energies. I believe that we as human beings interact with these Earth energies and that we need them for our health, balance and spiritual growth. This belief ties in with research showing that when at least 1 percent of the population of a city does transcendental meditation, the crime rate in that city will decrease.[1] Most likely we are talking about a similar phenomenon.

Meditation improves and expands the existing energy that supports our well-being. Our research indicates that the natural Earth energies in cities are strongly depleted.[2] Consequently, these natural Earth energies

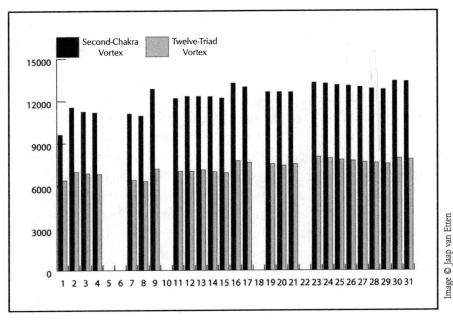

Fig. 33. This graph shows the measurements of the size of two vortexes taken over the course of one month near our house where we held weekly meditations on day 2, 9, 16, 23 and 30.

insufficiently support us in living healthy and balanced lives. Through meditation, these conditions of the Earth energy systems improve considerably, resulting in less crime. Using crystal skulls to support these meditations will increase the effects.

The Effects of Crystal Skulls on Human Beings

Many people who work with crystal skulls believe that the skulls have an effect on their health and well-being. However, what these effects are is not very clear. Is the increase in well-being a consequence of meditation, or do crystal skulls directly influence health and well-being? As far as I know, there are no in-depth studies on the effects crystal skulls have on us. There are, however, some initial studies that help us to get at least some impressions about the effects of crystal skulls on human beings. I would like to summarize the information that is available at this time.

In 1999, I attended a crystal skull gathering in Las Vegas where the speaker, Joshua Shapiro, brought his crystal skull Portal de Luz, a wonderful contemporary crystal skull. In many ways, it was an interesting gathering for me, because it was the first time I brought out in public the crystal skulls I had at that time. I brought Sam (my human-sized clear quartz skull), Aron (a very clear, almost human-sized smoky quartz skull), and Lanara (a three-inch clear quartz skull made by the same carver as Portal de Luz).

During the gathering, there was the possibility to get your aura photographed using Kirlian photography. I had one photo of my aura taken with Aron and one with Sam. I was not meditating with the skulls at that moment; I just took them on my lap one at a time. When the photo with Aron was taken, there was a lot of white light on the aura photo. The person who owned the Kirlian camera said that she had never seen this before. Interestingly, this light disappeared when the second photo with Aron was taken. As somebody noted, a signal needs to be given only once. The interpretation of those present was that this was a strong invitation to work with crystal skulls. Although the follow-up photos did not show the light again, with both Aron and Sam there was an improvement of my aura. As it was summarized by the person explaining the aura photos, they showed more of who I am and more clearly what my qualities are.

The results of my photos triggered the interest of several people, and they wanted their aura photos to be made first without and then while holding a crystal skull. When people picked up a skull they felt attracted to, the colors of their aura changed considerably. But if they were given a skull they did not make an immediate connection with, there was either no change or hardly any change in the colors of their aura. These experiences suggest that the degree of connection determines the effect crystal skulls have on people.

Although these experiences inspired me to find out more about the effects crystal skulls have on people, it took several years before I actually did more research. By that time, Jeanne and I had over a hundred skulls, yet my favorite skull to do research with was and still is Sam. In these first studies, I used RFI™ (see chapter 5) . To study the aura and chakras, the energies of forty points around the human body were measured according to a standard protocol. In this system, electromagnetic energies in the range of 1 MHz to 3 GHz were measured. The electromagnetic energies were divided into energy bands, and these energy bands correlate with one of the fifteen colors that this system uses. This means that each color has different energy bands. It also means that the qualities associated with the different colors can exist at different levels of vibration. Based on the agreement RFI™ researchers have with ITEM (Innovation Technologies and Energy Medicine), it is not possible to publish both the frequencies and the colors, so a researcher has to make a choice.

I tested a total of six people. People were tested before and after sitting with Sam for fifteen minutes. All people tested were used to meditating with crystal skulls and were able to make a deep connection with Sam, although the depth of the connection varied. A similar pattern was revealed in all test persons. Although the results were too limited and the variations too large to allow for more than general statements, it was remarkable to see that the overall physical and psychological condition improved. All systems became more stabilized and people became more relaxed.

The changes in the chakras were even more interesting. Before sitting with Sam, all the people tested showed frequencies related to the chakras that indicated they were more in a survival strategy mode than connected to their essence. But after sitting with Sam, the chakras showed the qualities and abilities of the people that reflected their essence. Although the degree of change varied per person, the general pattern was the same.

Let me give an example of one person to illustrate this. Gary has been a professional communicator most of his life. When I measured him before sitting with Sam, his chakras clearly reflected this (see Table 5).

Indicated here are the colors that relate to certain frequencies. In this case, the colors are more helpful in understanding what happened than the frequencies themselves. The meaning of each color for each chakra is mentioned in Table 5 as well.

Gary: Professional Communicator	Before Sitting with Sam	After Sitting with Sam
Chakra 1 Root Chakra	**Blue:** The deepest identity is being a communicator and the physical expression is on some expression or medium of communication.	**Gold:** The deepest identity is being a spiritual healer and the focus is on making connections between the physical and spiritual realms.
Chakra 2 Sacral Chakra	**Navy:** Leadership issues in life or in relationships need to be or are now being healed or resolved.	**Purple:** Intellectual issues in life or in relationships need to be or are being resolved.
Chakra 3 Solar Plexus	**Blue:** Communication issues affect the way you handle stress and your state of mind. Good communication makes you calm and comfortable.	**Orchid:** You have a calm and peaceful state of mind and you deal effectively with stress through spiritual emphasis.
Chakra 4 Heart Chakra	**Blue:** You are open in expression and communication, and emotions are also focused on communication issues.	**Purple:** The way you experience emotions is generally a function of how well you are able to intellectualize or rationalize a situation.
Chakra 5 Throat Chakra	**Navy:** You exert your intelligence, leadership and control over situations through your communication skills.	**Blue:** There is a healthy flow of communicative energies moving through your system.
Chakra 6 Third Eye	**Orchid:** The mental and psychic capacities are primarily focused on the acquisition and understanding of truth in all endeavors.	**Burgundy:** Mental and psychic capacities are in tune with human instincts and earthly consciousness.
Chakra 7 Crown Chakra	**Yellow:** The highest purpose and predominant spiritual priorities involve the experience of stability and happiness.	**Rose:** The highest purpose and predominant spiritual priorities involve the experience of entertainment, romance and sensuality.

Table 5. Through RFI™, I obtained colors connected to the chakras of a test person to compare the conditions before and after sitting with the crystal skull Sam.

The purpose is not to present a complete analysis of the results but in this case to focus on one aspect only, which is communication. Communication has been the main aspect in Gary's life. In the RFI™ system, blue is the color of communication. Before sitting with Sam, the color blue was found in the first, third and fourth chakras. This means he believes that communication is his identity. For him, good communication is a very important way to deal with the stress and state of his mind, but also with his emotions. The color navy in the fifth chakra indicated that he tends to use communication to be in control in order to prevent unpleasant situations.

After sitting with Sam, Gary connected with a deeper identity that felt truer for him: that of the spiritual healer. He used the wisdom aspects more (purple). Now the only chakra that had blue was the fifth chakra. This means that he is using his wonderful communication skills in a healthy and balanced way. He no longer needs communication as a way to survive in this world. Gary recognized the old part and the longing for the new part. This example clearly demonstrates the effect a crystal skull can have on a person.

Joshua Shapiro mentions research done through testing meridians with different meridian stress test systems.[3] These systems are all based on the same principle: They measure potential differences between a fixed point on the skin and different meridian points. These points can be measured before and after touching or meditation with a crystal skull. They did tests with contemporary, old and ancient crystal skulls, and compared quartz crystal skulls with pieces of quartz. They found that it is important for a person to connect with a crystal skull (in their case, through meditation while holding the crystal skull) to achieve the most optimal effect. People with a lot of experience with crystal skulls could more easily connect with them through touch. However, for proper comparison, it was better to meditate. The results showed that meditation with a crystal skull improved the condition of the test persons in most cases, although a few exceptions were found. They also noticed that when they worked with a contemporary skull that was used frequently (Portal de Luz), the results were comparable with those of an ancient skull.[4]

In general, the results Joshua Shapiro describes are in alignment with the impressions we got from our preliminary studies. Crystal skulls have positive effects on people when they really connect with them. They improve health and help people to connect deeper with their own essence.

Shapiro also describes experiments with different systems of aura measurements. Again the subjects worked with Joshua's contemporary crystal skull Portal de Luz. With every system, the same results were achieved. The crystal skull Portal de Luz improved the health of all people tested.[5]

Summarizing, we can say that all the preliminary studies give the same indication: crystal skulls have a positive effect on human beings. A lot more research needs to be done to understand this phenomenon better and to see how crystal skulls can be used in the most optimal way to support healing processes and to help people to connect more with their true authentic selves.

Crystal Skulls and Meditation

Most people will say that for them the preferred way to connect with crystal skulls is by meditating with them. Others find it is easier to connect through scrying, which is also called crystal-ball gazing. Other people like to go into a trance state and channel information from or through the crystal skull. Interestingly, whatever method a person uses, it goes back to the same principle. Before we look at that principle, let us look first at meditation.

There are many methods of meditation. Many books have been written on the subject, and many other books discuss meditation as part of their subject matter. In the different systems, the emphasis on certain aspects of meditation varies or even differs completely. Postures, breathing, mantras, candles, music and many other tools are mentioned to improve your meditation. Many people believe that a meditation is good when they "do not think" and get frustrated when they still have not been able to stop the thinking (the "monkey mind"). We see the same frustration during the crystal skull meditations at our house. We often hear people share that they felt the meditation was less good because there were so many thoughts.

This is not the place to go too deeply into details, but I would like to summarize a few points that hopefully will make your meditation easier, more fun and less a subject of judgment. Let us look first at what the principle of meditation is.

Scientific research has shown that the activities in our brain can be separated into four main states. Each of these brain states can be recognized by the frequencies the brain emits in that state (the activity); these brain-wave frequencies can be expressed in hertz (cycles per second). There are four frequency ranges that represent different states of our brain activity and also different states of awareness. These four states can be described as follows:

* **Beta state:** This state shows brain waves in the range from 12 Hz up to 30 Hz, although some researchers go as high as 40 Hz. These are the fastest frequencies and the patterns are generally very irregular. These are the brain waves of alertness, concentration and cognition. This state is associated with focused attention, peak concentration, clear thinking, processing visual information, hand-eye coordination, and also anxiety and worry, and fight or flight activity (heightened alertness). For most people, this is the dominant state of their brain waves during the day.

* **Alpha state:** The brain waves in this state have a frequency range from 8 to 12 Hz. Here the patterns are more regular than with beta waves. The keywords are relaxation, visualization and creativity. Its attributes are deep relaxation, detached awareness, non-drowsy, alert, reflective and contemplative, an open mental focus and introspective. This is the link from conscious beta (focused attention) to unconscious theta and higher conscious delta (deeper states of

awareness). When you sit quietly watching the sunset, the frequen
cies of your brain activity most likely move into the alpha state.

* **Theta state:** In this state, the brain waves range from 4 to 8 Hz.
Keywords are meditation, intuition and memory. This is also called
the waking dream state, and some call this the unconscious mind
function. This state is found while in deep meditation and during
dowsing, but also when we drift off to sleep, when we dream and
after we come out of the delta state. This is the subconscious connection to the higher conscious and the akashic records. It is the
state that leads to self-healing. Theta has been identified as the gateway to learning and memory. You need this state to connect on a
deeper level with, for example, crystal skulls and Earth energies.

* **Delta state:** This state has the lowest frequencies, ranging from
0.5 to 4 Hz. This state is defined as the higher conscious mind. It
acts as a radar or unconscious scanning device for intuition (hunch
or sixth sense), instinctive action, inner knowing and deep psychic
awareness. Some people call it the gateway to the soul. Normally
this state is only found in deep dreamless sleep. Neurons that are
not involved in the processing of information are all firing at the
same time. Certain frequencies in the delta range also trigger the
release of human growth hormone, so this state is beneficial for healing and regeneration.

Summarizing, we can say that the delta state is the state of deep dreamless sleep, whereas the beta state is the state of the normal day activities. It
has been shown that many types of meditation bring you into both the
alpha and theta states. While falling asleep you are in alpha, then in theta
(dreaming) and finally you move into delta (dreamless sleep).

What does this mean in relation to crystal skull meditations? In the
first place, we can see that an important aspect is relaxation. When we
have a concern that a meditation is not working, this very concern keeps

us mainly in the beta frequencies and we cannot move into the alpha state. For that reason, I do not pay so much attention to a specific posture. To me it is more important that a person feels comfortable, which makes it easier to relax. Once in alpha, most people move quite easily into theta. Then we are already in a meditative state. This is also the state in which we can connect with information through senses other than the five physical senses. It is the first step toward getting insights about ourselves and others. Meditation is, in fact, nothing more than relaxing to be able to move into the lower frequency states of the mind. The deeper the meditation, the lower the frequencies will be. Ultimately we can even move into the delta state.

The meditative state can be used in different ways. In the first place, meditation helps a person to relax and move into a state of tranquillity. This is a state in which your system regenerates and balances itself, and healing takes place. The meditative state can be used to find answers to questions or to find solutions for challenging situations.

When you meditate with a crystal skull, you can use the meditative state to obtain information about the crystal skull, its history and its energies. The intent you set before going into meditation will direct what will happen during the meditation. During your meditation, you may feel that you have gotten your answer and you can move to the next question. This requires the ability to use the beta frequency without moving out of the theta. Once you have acquired this skill through practice, you can combine beta (asking a question) with theta and delta (getting insights and answers).

When you go into meditation with a certain question in mind, you may open yourself for a flow of information that might come from your higher self, from angels, from guides or from other beings. It is this process that can lead to automatic writing or to channeling words or images. When channeling, it is important to feel whether the source is from beings of light and is connected with love.

Many people ask what they need to do when thoughts come up during the meditation. You can recognize when there is a thought and observe whether the thought is related to the intent set for the meditation. If the thought is related to the intent, allow it to unfold, explore it. If the thought is not related to the intention of the meditation, you can choose not to pay attention to it. If you give a thought energy or attention, it will grow. When thoughts get stronger, you have left the theta state and gone back into the beta state; you are no longer in a meditative state. To prevent this from happening, focus on something else—for example, on the crystal skull you have in your hand, on your breathing, on a mantra or on music, whatever will work for you. When you meditate with a certain focus, bring back your attention to that focus and continue your meditation.

Some people complain that they fall asleep during meditation. Especially when you are tired, that will easily occur when you relax. As you may have understood from the description, the theta state is both a meditative state and the dream state during our sleep. These two states are close together. Both in the meditative state and in the dream state, we access our unconsciousness. We still process on an unconscious level whatever the crystal skull has set into motion, even when we "fall asleep." In other words, the time is never wasted.

Realizing that theta is also the dream state helps us to understand that much of what we perceive during a meditation may come from our unconscious mind. That means that much of what we receive in meditation is probably at least partly symbolic, like in dreams. Therefore, it is wise to be careful with your interpretations.

There is a reason why we are often challenged by thoughts during our meditations. Especially when people meditate with crystal skulls or other objects, they like to know what happens during a meditation, to understand their experiences. In that case, we need a certain amount of beta activity in order to perceive what happens during a meditation and what information comes through. When people cannot remember what happened during the meditation and they obviously were not asleep, most likely their beta activity may have stopped almost completely. To be in a state of theta/delta is to be in a state of ultimate silence, a state of being. This is the state mystics and certain spiritual teachers talk about.

It is a state of nothing and everything, a place beyond identity. Crystal skulls can be a tool to achieve this state as long as we are clear that this is our purpose.

Meditation is to a certain degree a delicate balance of different brain activities. For that reason, the quality of our meditations may fluctuate easily. The most important part is to stay relaxed, to allow anything to happen and to be without judgment. That makes it easier to stay sufficiently deep in the theta state.

Whether we meditate, whether we tune in to something or whether we do a reading of the energies of a person, we need to be in a state of theta or delta. Psychic ability is the ability to go into the theta and/or delta state and to be aware of the information that comes in. At the same time, we need to be sufficiently connected to the beta state to give form or words to the information that comes through.

Using crystal skulls for meditation helps us to stay in the theta and/or delta state. That helps us to have all the benefits of meditation (improved well-being and health), and it also opens us for the possibility to receive information. The meditative state may be the only way to resolve the riddles of the crystal skulls.

CRystal Skulls and Empowerment

Empowerment sounds like a strange subject in a crystal skull book: What relationship do crystal skulls have with empowerment? My answer is, a lot. In the time I have been active in the crystal skull world, I have seen and observed people's reaction to crystal skulls. I have heard people talk about crystal skulls in various ways, which has prompted me to write this small but, to my opinion, very important section. I am very aware that some people may not agree with my view on empowerment and disempowerment. Feel for yourself what your understanding of empowerment will be.

Crystal skulls are wonderful gifts and creations. I am aware that every creation on whatever level has consciousness, and they are wonderful tools. For me the word "tool" refers to anything that can help us to understand who we are. To make a bold statement: The whole universe is a tool to help us understand our true authentic self. Crystal skulls are an aspect of that universe and, as such, are tools.

In our search for who we truly are, we learn to take full responsibility for every action, every feeling and every thought. This means we can never say that such and such told us and that's the reason why we do what we do. When we do so, we give our power away to "such and such." It does not matter who we believe has told us, whether it be a teacher, a guru, an angel or a crystal skull. If they are truly beings of light, they will never temper with our free will. Beings of light will always respect our free will. This does not mean that we do not receive signs or signals from wherever they come from. But we have to make a choice whether what we hear is in alignment with what we feel as our highest truth or whether it is not. This is how we learn to understand and express who we truly are.

Going back to crystal skulls, it is important to *never* give our power away to crystal skulls. "The skull says" can never be the only reason why we make a certain choice. If we follow what the skull says without taking responsibility for our choice, we are disempowering ourselves. Only when "what the skull says" feels in alignment with our highest truth can we accept it and act accordingly. Then our interaction and relationship with our crystal skulls is empowering. Taking full responsibility for every choice we make helps us to grow and to connect deeper with who we are.

Crystal Skulls and Energy Fields

Most people work with crystal skulls one at a time. They interact with a crystal skull in whatever way feels appropriate. When talking about crystal skulls, generally people talk about their personal experiences with each individual skull. Books about crystal skulls mainly describe personal interactions with particular crystal skulls.

Another way to use crystal skulls is in ceremonies. A number of ancient crystal skulls—such as Max, ShaNaRa and E.T.—have been involved in ceremonies led by Native people. The crystal skulls were part of these ceremonies, but as far as I know, they have never been the main focus of them. Contemporary crystal skulls have also been used to support ceremonies and events. The facilitator's intent determines in what way a crystal skull will contribute during a ceremony. I have heard people describe ceremonies where crystal skulls were present as powerful. However, ceremonies can also be powerful without the presence of crystal skulls. To understand the contribution of crystal skulls, those leading the ceremony would have to share how they used the crystal skulls during that ceremony, and most ceremonial leaders do not easily talk about the details of their ceremonies.

Crystal skulls reflect the energy of their environment. Through their interaction with their environment, crystal skulls create an energy field. Our intent is part of that environment and consequently codetermines the quality of the created energy field of a crystal skull.

From the moment Jeanne and I started teaching workshops, we used crystal skulls for support. We always mention to the participants that we like to use crystal skulls to help us hold the energy field that we as facilitators cocreate together with the group in order to optimally support what we want to achieve during a particular workshop. I often say jokingly, "The crystal skulls help a lazy man." By using them, we do not have to work so hard. When we use crystal skulls, the field is much stronger than without them. Jeanne and I also create energy fields as a basis for group meditations.

I would like to give a couple of examples to help you understand what type of energy fields we have created over time and how to create them. First I feel I should mention that creating energy fields is Jeanne's specialty. She has become a true master in creating different energy fields, much to the delight of myself and the participants of our weekly meditation evenings.

Crystal skulls can be used to create any type of energy field you wish. There are, however, a number of factors that play a role. One factor is the size of the crystal skull. The second is the degree of activation of the crystal skull. The third factor is the number of crystal skulls that are used. And the fourth is the clarity of intent.

I have mentioned that for individual use, the size of a crystal skull does not really matter. Smaller crystal skulls can even have an advantage above larger ones: they are not so heavy, which makes it more convenient to hold them and transport them. Small crystal skulls can even be put into your pocket or small handbag.

When we use a crystal skull for the creation of an energy field, the size of the skull can become important. The size of an energy field that can be created by a crystal skull grows exponentially with the size of the crystal skull. This means that if the size of the field is important, than the size of the crystal skull as well as its level of activation is a factor in choosing which skulls are to be used. Anyone who knows how to dowse is able to determine the size of the energy field that is created by a certain crystal skull after it has been activated as fully as possible.

Let me give a few examples of measurements of energy fields created by some of our contemporary crystal skulls. A two-inch clear quartz skull creates an energy field with a diameter of 10 yards. A clear quartz crystal skull of three inches creates an energy field with a diameter of 24 yards. Whereas the energy field of a six-inch clear smoky quartz skull has a diameter of 280 yards. The given sizes of the energy fields clearly show that even a crystal skull of two inches covers an area the size of a large room. A crystal skull of two inches can easily fulfill all personal needs and even those of small groups. None of the crystal skulls we used for the measurements was fully activated. They had reached the level of twelve polyhedral fields (PHFs), but not all twelve levels within the twelfth PHF had been activated.

When we use fully activated crystal skulls to create energy fields, we see the same pattern: as we use larger skulls, the crystal skull field increases exponentially. However, the size of the field is much larger than when using less activated crystal skulls. For example, a 2.4-inch crystal skull from Nepal creates a field with a diameter of 40 yards, whereas a 3-inch clear quartz skull (Ti) creates a field with a radius of 120 yards. Sam, a clear quartz human-sized fully activated contemporary crystal skull creates a field with a diameter of 2 miles.

For comparison, I estimated through dowsing the size of the energy fields of some crystal skulls that are considered to be ancient. For example, Max creates an energy field with a diameter of 2.4 miles, whereas the Mitchell-Hedges Skull creates a field of 10 miles. The size of the field that is created by activating the Mitchell-Hedges Skull is of another level than that of Max and Sam.

The only written record on the size of the energy field of crystal skulls comes from Nick Nocerino. In *Mysteries of the Crystal Skulls Revealed*, he explains that ancient crystal skulls interact with the human mind and create a wall of energy that extends high up and spreads over a large distance. He mentions that the Mayan Skull creates a field that stretches nearly a mile.[6] This means that the diameter of the field is around two miles. This is similar to what I have found for Sam and close to that of Max. He also talks about the existence of an energy field created by the Mitchell-Hedges Skull. He mentions that when he was two blocks away, the wall of energy was still moving away, indicating that the field was still growing. This time he did not measure the distance over which the field eventually spread.[7]

The third factor that determines the size of the crystal skull energy field is the number of crystal skulls used to create the energy field. Our group of over 120 crystal skulls sitting in a dormant state has a field with a diameter of 0.7 miles. However, when fully activated, they create a field with a diameter of 8.2 miles. If we use three two-inch contemporary crystal skulls, they can create an energy field with a diameter of 120 yards.

The last factor is the factor of intent. As we mentioned earlier, the person who induces the activation determines the level of activation. It is the level of consciousness in which that person is functioning at the moment of activation that determines the level of activation. A person who cannot activate the full potential of the crystal skull or the group of crystal skulls will create energy fields that are smaller than those who can.

It may have become clear that when a person wants to use crystal skulls for energy support during a ceremony with a large group or to have a meditation during a large event, the size of the crystal skulls, the number of crystal skulls and the level of their activation, as well as the facilitator's ability to activate, are all important. They all need to be taken into account to enable an optimal result.

Although the size of the energy field you may want to create with crystal skulls is important, even more important is the quality of the field. It is important to be clear about what kind of energy field you want to create. With crystal skulls, you can create any energy field you can imagine. The only limitation is the limitation of your imagination. This may sound far-fetched to some of you as it initially did for me. Working with Jeanne for almost nine years has clearly shown me and those participating in our crystal skull meditations and workshops that it is truly possible to create any energy field we want. We can even do the same without crystal skulls. However, with crystal skulls it is easier and in general the fields are larger and stronger and consequently easier to perceive by the people who are participating. When we create energy fields with crystal skulls, this helps us to go deeper into meditation. Crystal skulls also reflect more clearly the meaning that the created field has for us personally.

Let me give a few examples of the fields Jeanne has created over time. We have experienced dolphin and whale energy fields. She has created an energy field of archangels in general and those of certain archangels, such as Michael, Raphael, Gabriel and Uriel. We have worked with the energies of Quan Yin and Mother Mary. She has created energy fields that resonated with each of the chakras, and in that way we worked with all seven chakras. We have worked with water that has been charged on certain vortexes or on certain sacred sites. We've even worked with pinecones that were found in the energies of a portal to Tau Ceti, giving people a very special experience. These examples show that there is no limitation in what you can do. Try it out for yourself and enjoy the journey.

I would like to add one piece of advice: Especially in the beginning, use tools that help you focus on the type of field you want to create. For example, if you want to create a dolphin energy field, use images of dolphins, carvings or maybe even a piece of dolphin bone. It helps the creator of the energy field to connect more deeply with the dolphins and therefore the intent can be set more clearly and fully. Use your own imagination to see what works best for you. It does not matter *what* you put next to the crystal skulls to help you focus on the field you want to create; what matters is what helps you the most to connect with the field you want to create.

What is important is not the crystal skulls themselves or the field that you want to create. What is important is what you learn about yourself when you do so. What do the different fields reflect to you? What do you feel, what do you experience, what images do you get? The true purpose is to understand who you are. Creating these fields is a helpful means to obtain these insights.

The Collective Crystal Skull Field

So far we have talked about energy fields that are induced by our intent and through our interactions with the crystal skulls. There is, however, another type of energy field that is formed by all crystal skulls together and that contains all the energies and qualities crystal skulls have—as I described earlier, I call this the collective crystal skull (energy) field. Again, this collective crystal skull field is the sum of all the energies that the crystal skulls radiate and have radiated, and in that sense, it is comparable to Jung's human collective (un)consciousness field.

My first understanding of the collective crystal skull field was that this field was rather homogenous, with all kinds of frequencies that dynamically interact. My theory was that, depending on the state of activation

Image © Jaap van Etten

Fig. 34. The shape of the collective crystal skull field.

and the quality of the material the crystal skull was made from, each crystal skull resonated with certain energies from this field and, of course, contributed to that field when somebody activated it and worked with it. Although most of this seems to be true, the collective crystal skull field is less homogenous than I initially thought. In a meditation I received an image—which I fine-tuned during several consecutive meditations—that helps us to understand the energetic dynamics of this field [see Fig. 34].

The image shows that the collective crystal skull energy field has four subfields, which are interconnected and interact with each other. Each of the four subfields holds energies of different types and frequencies. They relate to the four types of crystal skulls that are described in Part 1. The contemporary crystal skulls form the base, the fully activated crystal skulls (the old and ancient crystal skulls) form the second layer, the singing crystal skulls form the third layer and the original crystal skulls, the fourth (top) layer.

The energies of the contemporary crystal skulls are represented by the basic layer. This layer contains all the energies (all the frequencies) of all contemporary crystal skulls, independent of their level of activation. The energies of the fully activated crystal skulls are represented by the two lower layers. This means that fully activated crystal skulls include the energies contemporary crystal skulls have. There are additional energies and frequencies contained within the second layer that are specific for the fully activated crystal skulls. Most of these energies (and information) were programmed into these crystals skulls in unique ways a long time ago. They are waiting for us to learn how to retrieve this information.

The singing crystal skulls are represented by the third layer. They contain all energies of the first two layers plus the third layer, which contains energies that make the singing crystal skulls unique. We are learning how to access the energies and information of this third layer. The original crystal skulls are energetically characterized by the top layer, but they actually contain the energies of all four layers indicated in the image. They are also directly connected with the sources that have created them. This connection is indicated by the vortex on top of the fourth layer.

A vortex is a place where energy and thus information is exchanged. It is actually a doorway that allows energy exchange and communication in both directions. Those who work with crystal skulls can use this doorway to connect with other-dimensional and even extraterrestrial consciousness. At the same time, these consciousnesses can use the crystal skulls to connect with us. It is because of these connections that people sometimes say that a crystal skull is from Sirius, or from the Pleiades, or from Orion. We will look more extensively at these extra-terrestrial connections in Part 3.

The strongest interaction between subfields takes place between the first two layers of the contemporary and the fully activated crystal skulls.

The skulls of these two layers are all carved from existing crystals, which makes them different from the skulls of layers three and four. At this moment, the number of contemporary crystal skulls grows rapidly and the number of people working with them increases. Consequently, the field of the contemporary crystal skulls is quickly growing in strength, though not necessarily in its range of frequencies. Most contemporary crystal skulls are not yet fully activated and their energies are indicated in the lowest subfield by the dark band at the bottom.

However, there is a growing understanding of crystal skulls and how to activate them, which will increase the number of contemporary crystal skulls that become more or even fully activated. This is indicated by the area of overlap in energies between the existing fully activated (old and ancient) crystal skulls and the contemporary crystal skulls. This overlap will become larger as more contemporary crystal skulls become fully activated and more information gets programmed into them. At the same time, there will always be a unique part of the old and ancient fully activated crystal skulls that differs from fully activated contemporary crystal skulls. This unique part has been formed by special programming by the ancients and by the different people who have worked with these skulls over time.

The unique energies of the third layer are represented by the six extra PHFs that were described earlier. As we will see in the next part of the book, they contain energies that have been induced through the processes of morphocrystallic generation and morphocrystallic transformation.

This image of the total collective crystal skull field has given me a better understanding of the energies of the different groups and the interactions between them. In theory, a person can connect with an original skull while using a contemporary crystal skull. This connection is possible because all layers are interconnected. However, the likelihood that a person makes such a connection is very low. The energies of the lower subfield and the higher subfield have such a big difference in frequencies that the probability of creating a direct connection between a contemporary skull and an original or a singing skull is small. Nonetheless, it is possible and it may explain why certain people have such profound experiences when they connect the first time with a contemporary crystal skull.

The Effects of Crystal Skull Fields on the Environment

We have seen that we can create energy fields with crystal skulls that cover quite large areas. The question may arise concerning what effect such fields might have on the energies of the environment. There is not a simple answer to this question. A great deal depends on the frequencies of the energies in the created field. Different frequencies will have different effects on different systems or interact with different systems. Earlier we saw that crystal skulls have powerful effects on Earth energies.

We have studied the effects of crystal skulls on specific Earth energy systems. So far, however, we have only studied a small part of the total number of Earth energy systems. Much more research will be needed to get a deeper understanding, both of the Earth energy systems and of the effect that the crystal skulls have on these systems. Initial research (reported in chapter 5) indicates that crystal skulls, once activated, greatly contribute in the creation of an energetic environment that supports us by improving our health and our emotional balance and stability.

Every time we create a crystal skull energy field, it will affect all people who are within that field. For example, when we have a crystal skull meditation with the more than 120 crystal skulls in our house, it generates a field that spreads many miles. Everyone within that field is affected, although the degree of the effect depends on many factors. However, there will always be a positive effect.

Studies have shown that meditation positively affects the environment. These studies have been done with practitioners of transcendental meditation. As I mentioned earlier, results show that in large cities in which about 1 percent of the population regularly meditated, the crime rate significantly decreased.[8] This indicates that meditation has a positive effect on people and that they do not have to be aware that these meditations are happening. I believe the same is true for the energy fields created when people meditate with or activate crystal skulls.

The fact that crystal skull energy fields have such a powerful effect makes it even more important to have a clear intent when working with the skulls. The more clearly the *intent comes from love and respect for ourselves and everyone around us*, the more powerful the positive effects on the environment will be.

CHAPTER 7

Crystal Skulls and Channeled Information

In general, I am very careful with channeled information. I am open to all information, though I always check to see whether I resonate with that information before I use it. In this chapter, I would like to present the channeled information I am aware of that feels relevant within the context of this book. Hopefully, this will give some additional views that may be helpful for the reader to get a deeper understanding of the crystal skull phenomenon. I will give additional comments on the content of the channeling where it feels appropriate.

The Mitchell-Hedges Skull through Carole Davis

There is a difference between channeling about crystal skulls and channeling a crystal skull. An example of the latter type of channeling has been published in a book called *The Skull Speaks Through Carole Davis*, where trance channel Carole Davis channels information locked in the Mitchell-Hedges Skull. The book contains the transcriptions of nine channelings, spanning from May 9, 1982, to October 21, 1984.[1]

Davis is very clear that she is not certain the information came directly from the skull. She also states that she does not pretend the information is correct. However, there is information in this book that

I feel is worth looking into. During the first channeling session, a suggestion is given that the origin of the Mitchell-Hedges Skull was as the great crystal of Atlantis. The great crystal and other crystals were created with "mind" and grown in the time of Atlantis.[2]

This book is a worthwhile read, although it is not easy to find as it is out of print. It gives information about the origins of our planet and of the human race—information that may help us in the future.

Mahasamatman through Kathleen Murray

Another example of a book that came into being through channeling is *The Divine Spark of Creation: The Crystal Skull Speaks,* from channel Kathleen Murray.[3] Kathleen is the keeper of a crystal skull called Mahasamatman. As she describes it, "Mahasamatman was logged into physical reality at the beginning of 1995."[4] Together they have been doing Earth work, attuning the Earth to the vibrations of planetary and stellar resonances. Mahasamatman is here to voice to the world, through Kathleen as a channel, the work that crystal skulls and Mahasamatman in particular are here to do.

Mahasamatman is considered to be a living consciousness that regards himself as a vehicle for a group of universal intelligences who call themselves the Galactic Masters. In the introduction of the book, it clearly states that, "All the crystal skulls, whether deemed ancient or contemporary"—Mahasamatman regards himself as eternal, not ancient, and can be proven not to be contemporary—"are living consciousnesses—receivers and transmitters—vehicles inhabited by groups of universal intelligences."[5] Kathleen makes one statement in particular that has relevance for me. She says, "Through Mahasamatman shine the Stellar Rays, the team of Thirteen, which seeded humanity. As the stellar memory banks open to you, you will find your remembrances coming through."[6] We will come back to this statement and the meaning of it in Part 3.

Sandra Bowen and Michael Kant

Several channelings have been described in *Mysteries of the Crystal Skulls Revealed*.[7] I consider the channelings given by Sandra Bowen and Michael Kant especially interesting and, for those interested in crystal skulls, very worthwhile to read. In both channelings, there are several references to the legend of the thirteen crystal skulls.

Michael Kant is a conscious channel who has experienced many contacts with various spiritual beings, including extraterrestrials, angels and those of the solar hierarchy. He has had two conscious UFO experiences, one with beings from the Pleiades and one with the spaceship of Sananda. He is interested in Atlantean and sacred sciences, crystals, UFOs and light-based technologies.[8]

In an extensive interview, Kant gives a lot of information on crystal skulls, crystal technologies, lightships and much more.[9] Kant believes that the Mitchell-Hedges Skull was originally in one of the thirteen healing temples of Atlantis and that it is the skull of the female priestess Shee-thee-tra (who was killed during one of the last earthquakes on Atlantis) that was transformed into crystal.[10] When Kant talks about the "crystal skulls," he is referring to the thirteen crystal skulls produced through morphocrystallic generation, which were originally placed in the thirteen healing temples of Atlantis but are now located beneath the Potala in Tibet.[11]

Michael Kant introduced the term *morphocrystallic science*. This term refers to a technology that the Atlanteans used to create crystals and crystal skulls. One way is to create a thought form that functions as a matrix to create crystals or crystal skulls. This technique is called *morphocrystallic generation*. Another technique is the creation of crystals using an existing matrix of other materials, like the bone of a human skull—called *morphocrystallic transformation*. The technique of morphocrystallic transformation was used to create the Mitchell-Hedges Skull from the skull of the Atlantean priestess.[12]

Sandra Bowen is also a conscious channel. She receives messages from her "friends from space": Akbar and Josephat. The basic theme of the information that was given to her deals with the mission or spiritual work she agreed to do in relation to the crystal skulls. They explained that there was a plan involving many people on Earth, as well as extra-terrestrials, to bring all the ancient crystal skulls into alignment with thirteen special pyramids.[13]

In *Mysteries of the Crystal Skulls Revealed*, there is a chapter on Sandra Bowen in which channeled information is presented that was given to help Sandra access information in crystal skulls like the Mitchell-Hedges.[14] She was told that the sound of the human voice can help to access a skull's information.[15]

Sandra also works with the gold beings who work closely with the archangels and are as close to Source as the archangels are.[16] During the interview, Sandra also mentions the thirteen crystal skulls under the Potala in Tibet. However, she believes that these crystal skulls are moving from Tibet to the Four Corners region in the Southwest of the United States.[17]

Monitor through Harvey Grady

Monitor is channeled by Harvey Grady, who lives in Sedona, Arizona.[18] All questions and answers on the subject of crystal skulls date from the beginning of 2001.

Monitor shares that the shape of the skull initially had no meaning. Now, however, the shape of the skull symbolically represents the access each human has to knowledge and wisdom developed and maintained in the mental plane of the Earth. The skull reminds people that they can attune to the wisdom and knowledge that is available to those who seek it and can develop personal protocols to draw forth the information in a usable way. He states that in order to utilize a quartz crystal skull (he talks only about quartz), the person needs to link his or her mental body with the mental body of the quartz being. According to him, this can only happen with the permission of the quartz being.[19]

When a crystal skull has already been programmed with a particular belief system and protocol for use, a person is often required to learn that protocol before she can develop her own protocol. It is like computer software—a person needs to learn how to use the software before she can customize it.[20]

According to Monitor, there are safeguards placed around ancient crystal skulls and crystals. Those safeguards represent a structure of thought forms and imperatives that limit access to those who are devoted to altruism. They prevent access to those personalities that are selfish.[21] Old/ancient and contemporary skulls differ in that the ancient skulls have established protocols, whereas the contemporary skulls have more flexible protocols. Some of the crystal skulls have been created by extraterrestrials, in most cases by the Pleiadeans. They have been programmed to give access to Pleiadeans.[22]

On a question about polyhedral fields around crystals and crystal skulls and their function, Monitor answers: "The altruism of the crystals is highly developed. As human altruism approaches that level, the human/crystal bond becomes more profound. The energetic layers around and within a crystal reflects the various levels of substance and force present in the etheric, astral and mental bodies of the crystal. The layers are multiple for each crystal, yet the characteristic expressed by those separate layers of force can be qualified and developed in specific ways through mental impression."[23] This is greatly in alignment with what we shared about polyhedral fields earlier.

In general, the information given by Monitor is in alignment with what has been shared in this book. Although we are familiar with the fact that certain skulls are used as transmitters by other consciousness, such as the Pleiadeans [see Part 3], it is remarkable that the accent on the connection with the Pleiadeans is that strong. Monitor suggests that crystal skulls were created by a pre-Mayan race.[24] It is believed that the Mayan ancestors were from the Pleiades. Many Native

American tribes also hold that belief. Perhaps this is what Monitor is referring to.

Lazaris through Jach Pursel

The information presented here is from a lecture Lazaris gave in 1984 called *Crystals: The Mystery & Magic of "Ancient One" Crystals and Crystal Skulls.*[25] Whereas Monitor focuses on the Pleiades, Lazaris focuses on Sirius. Lazaris talks about the Ancients—according to him, there are fourteen races of Ancients. The most ancient are the translucent beings from Sirius, who are also called the Beings of Light. They formed on Earth the Lemurian Dreamers, and some of them became the Guardians of the Crystals in the Atlantean times. Lazaris describes that there are Ancients working through certain crystals, which he calls Ancient crystals.[26]

Lazaris sees the true crystal skulls more as a crystal skull consciousness. In Lemurian times, this crystal skull consciousness was brought to Earth by the Sirians in the form of crystals, not so much in the form of crystal skulls. The function of crystals with crystal skull consciousness had some similarity with that of record-keeping crystals. Lazaris prefers to call them "witnesses," as they were used to "witness" events. The smaller ones were carried to the events to record the event, and the information could then be brought into larger crystals for storage.[27] Although I believe that crystal skulls can be used as witnesses, I have difficulty with his statement that crystal skull consciousness was brought to Earth in the form of crystals.

According to Lazaris, in Atlantis things became more physically represented. So during the time of Atlantis, the crystals with crystal skull consciousness were carved into the form of a skull. They were also used in Atlantis as witnesses. Especially during the time of Lemuria, crystals with crystal skull energy/consciousness were used for healing as well.[28]

Lazaris also mentions that crystal skulls can be teleporting devices. Basically, you can teleport from one skull to another. This is mainly emotional and mental teleportation, and not so much physical teleportation, although that is also possible.[29]

Crystal skulls are also windows to the future. It is possible to connect to future selves. In general, Lazaris sees crystal skulls as more dynamic than crystals and also more "talkative." He mentions one special characteristic: crystal skulls drain negative energy.[30] This comment ties in with my experience that crystal skulls do not take on negative energy. Therefore, a crystal skull does not need to be "cleared" or "cleaned" unless it is programmed through intent with negative energy.

Lazaris is very clear: Not all crystal skulls have the crystal skull energy! This statement can only be understood in the light of his belief that crystal skull consciousness is different from the energy and consciousness of crystal skulls.[31] As I mentioned earlier, I cannot resonate with this idea.

Lazaris makes an interesting statement. He says that he does not want to talk about the Mitchell-Hedges Skull and about the story of thirteen crystal skulls. He leaves it to others to believe what they choose to believe. Nevertheless, he mentions that the number thirteen is wrong. The true number should metaphorically be fourteen. He refers to the story of Osiris, who was cut into fourteen parts that were spread all over the world. The way he talks suggests that the story of Osiris metaphorically represents the story that when Atlantis was destroyed, the survivors spread into fourteen directions. He says that only thirteen places where the survivors went to are known and that one of the locations is "lost." According to Lazaris, the fourteen crystal skulls have an energy field that spans time and space, and the number fourteen refers to the fourteen races from Sirius.[32] We will come to the subject of the original skulls in Part 3.

Bashar through Darryl Anka

Of all the beings channeled, I resonate most with Bashar.[33] This does not mean that what he shares is always easy to understand in its fullness. Often there are layers of information in one answer, and sometimes the answer has more depth for those who asked the question. All the questions and answers I refer to below are from undated transcripts; this means that the date and location of the channeling cannot be given. However, most channelings were done in Los Angeles and are most likely from the early 1990s.

One question I posed to Bashar is about the origin of the crystal skulls and what their purpose is. In his answer, Bashar mentions that there are many crystal skulls, but he chooses to refer to the one that we associate with the Mayan civilization (I believe he refers to the Mitchell-Hedges Skull). He says it functioned as a model for the rearrangement of the energy pathways within the brain that allowed them (the Mayans) to connect with other-dimensional experiences of reality. He said that crystal skulls were left behind for other people to find to allow them to also enter this dimensional doorway. However, those guided to do so first must identify with the crystal skull. According to Bashar, when you identify yourself with the crystal skull, it will function as a symbolic reflector, an energizer, an accelerator, which will help you to blend with all aspects of yourself. That is the so-called "safeguard." If you cannot do the blending of all portions of your personality, you will not be able to enter the doorway. The reflector will bring up all issues (fears) that will prevent the blending of all aspects of you and consequently will prevent you from going through the doorway when you are not yet ready.

In answering a question about the thirteen skulls and their coming together, Bashar first makes a short comment that more than thirteen exist. Then he shares that bringing together different skulls is a symbolic reflection of different portions of the personality, forming a circle that will allow there to be an energizing, as well as the formation and the opening of a greater doorway to another dimensional experience of yourself through which you can step.

When Bashar is asked to comment on the statement that people believe that the origins of the crystal skulls are pre-Atlantean or even pre-Lemurian, he reacts by saying that there is some reality in the sense that it predates the Mayan. "It is mostly the idea of the technology itself and the utilization of that technology in that way that predated the arti-fact. It was simply that technology, that understanding, that informa-tion, that allowed that civilization to create such an artifact that carries with it a sense of ancientness about it by its very nature. Because of the blueprints it was fashioned from, it carries with it intrinsic connections to ancient times. This means that each artifact created in that manner would be perceived as ancient, meaning older than it physiologically is. In a sense, it is through the technology of its crafting. But it also is a dimensional doorway, an energy gate, which connects it to all places and all times. That makes it feel older." In another channeling, Bashar refers to the fact that dolphins know how to use the crystal skull as a doorway and can help us to reconnect with that idea.

In a personal channeling, I asked a question about crystal skulls and the doorways. I had felt that Bashar seemed to refer to the Mitchell-Hedges Skull and maybe to Max when he talked about dimensional doorways. However, I felt that contemporary crystal skulls could do the same. This was Bashar's response:

Bashar: "Of course. It depends upon the intention that's put into them and how, and in what reality and in what vibration they are created. Of course. As I said, it's a tool which means it's a per-mission slip. But it may be designed in a very specific way to key into a particular vibration a person feels they need to experience in order to give themselves permission to key into other dimen-sions. It's an intermediary. That's all it is. It's a medium. But yes, new ones can do the same."

My comment: It's the matter of the intent of the people that are now owning them and working with them.

Bashar: "Yes. Of course. Because the intent, in that sense as they are working, will guide them to create it in a way that cre-ates a specific vibration that is aligned with their intent."

Bashar is very clear that it is through intent that we can use the crystal skulls to access other dimensions, mainly other dimensions of consciousness. His comments also confirm that contemporary crystal skulls have the same potential as ancient ones. The difference is in the degree of activation and in the information that is stored in the skulls.

PART 3

The Thirteen Original Crystal Skulls

The legend of the thirteen crystal skulls has been clearly anchored in the minds of those interested in crystal skulls. This does not mean the story is very well-known, or that it is easy to separate fact from fantasy. It is a legend, and there is no proof that it is more than that. For some people, the legend is irrelevant, but for others, the story stirs something in them. The legend is often told in slightly different ways, and it is also included in the traditions of many Native people.

This story has fascinated me from the moment I first heard about it. It has become an important part of my journey with the crystal skulls. In this part of the book, I would like to share the stories presented by others. I would also like to give my version of the story and place it in a larger context.

First I would like to make a comment: The information I share consists of either my beliefs or those of others. As the reader, you need to feel whether you resonate with this information. It is wonderful if you can, and if you cannot, then simply see it as another belief that may be interesting to read about.

CHAPTER 8

Pursuing the Legend of the Thirteen Skulls

My Introduction to the Legend

The first time I came across the legend of the thirteen crystal skulls was in 1993. At that time, I was studying Native American medicine. As part of the study, I read *The Medicine Way* by Kenneth Meadows.[1] In the chapter on "Ancient Origins," I read that the people of the Cherokee Nation believe they originated in the Pleiades, which later I found to be a belief held by many Native tribes—not only from the Americas, but also tribes from Taiwan.[2] Kenneth Meadows mentions that there is a story amongst the Cherokee teachings that says there are twelve skulls, each fashioned from a piece of solid quartz crystal. What is said to be unusual about these skulls is not just that they are the size of a human skull but that the jaw is detachable and can move, and that they "speak" or "sing."[3]

Meadows got his information from Harley Swiftdeer, a Métis Cherokee medicine man. Swiftdeer explained that according to oral Cherokee teachings, the twelve skulls in ancient times were positioned in a circle around an amethyst crystal skull (the thirteenth crystal skull) and that eight crystal wands were placed within this arrangement, one for each of the cardinal (east, south, west, north) and noncardinal (southeast, southwest, northwest, northeast) directions. He said that each of these skulls was very old and each was like a holographic computer, which held information that had been programmed into it, including knowledge about the origins, purpose and destiny of humans as well as the so-called "mysteries of life."[4]

According to Swiftdeer, the singing skulls would one day be rediscovered and brought together for their collective knowledge to be made available, but men and women would have to be sufficiently evolved so that they would not misuse it. Swiftdeer told Kenneth Meadows that according to these ancient teachings, there were twelve planets in the cosmos inhabited by humans, and souls could travel around them as they evolved. There was a crystal skull for each of these planets. Kenneth Meadows wonders whether the story is far-fetched, but he then refers to the Mitchell-Hedges Skull, which he believes can be seen as a solid confirmation that the legend has some basis.[5]

I was fascinated by this story, but I had never heard of crystal skulls, so I soon forgot about it. In 1994, I visited Sedona, Arizona, and met my first crystal skull, as described in the introduction to this book. This experience did not immediately bring back the memory of what I had read in Kenneth Meadows' book; it only induced curiosity in general and a longing to work with a crystal skull. At that time, I lived in Holland, so the only way to work with a crystal skull was to have my "own" skull.

In June 1996, I became the caretaker of Sam (my human-sized clear quartz crystal skull). By that time, I had read many stories on crystal skulls in general and about the thirteen crystal skulls in particular. In *Mysteries of the Crystal Skulls Revealed*, there is a lot of information on the thirteen original skulls and variations on the theme.[6] I learned that not everyone believes there are only thirteen of these crystal skulls. Sandra Bowen talks about thirty-six crystal skulls, and Don Alejandro Cirilo Perez Oxlaj, a Mayan high priest, believes there are fifty-two original skulls.[7] I also have read about other numbers. I found the variety of stories rather confusing, and it felt for me that although there seemed to be an underlying myth or legend, every vision or imagination that is shared is only another belief. After all, there is no solid proof for any of these ideas.

Λdventure in the Sierras Madres

In 1996, I went to Mexico with three friends. Working off channeled information, we looked for possible remnants of Atlantis in the Sierras Madres, south of Durango. My friend Herman had asked me whether I had an interest in going to Mexico, showing me images of what we might discover, and I had felt a very strong energy telling me I needed to be part of this expedition. We prepared for almost two years before leaving for Mexico. We were forewarned that this trip would change our lives drastically, but this did not prevent us from looking forward to this adventure with high expectations.

The area in the Sierras was very remote, and although we knew the coordinates and had a GPS, we got lost in the mountains, unable to reach the point that had been indicated. We were guided to camp near a couple of old wooden houses where an extended family lived. They gave us permission to stay with them for as long as we wanted, and one of the men offered to help us. When he was told we were looking for a special place in the mountains, he nodded and said he knew the place. We wondered how he could know—the only thing we had mentioned was "a special place." To our utter surprise, he brought us straight to the location we had been looking for, a hike of several hours through the mountains.

The surprise heightened our expectations, but it was followed by a deep disappointment. We did not find any physical evidence of Atlantis. What we found, however, was a place which had such a special energy that it had a profound effect on me [see Plate 21]. I was emotional, I cried and I behaved irrationally. The whole time we were in that area, I kept feeling crystal skulls and I was convinced they were there somewhere in the mountains. I wondered whether this experience was the real reason I had to come to this remote location. I felt a strong desire to go into the mountains to search for the crystal skulls, but the area was extremely rough with deep ravines, which made it impossible to go and search. We went back to the Netherlands with mixed feelings. The other members were disappointed and felt we failed, but I went back wondering what happened at this special place, longing to go back one day to find the crystal skulls I was convinced were in that remote area.

The prediction turned out to be right: The lives of all four of us changed drastically in unexpected directions. It seems that the energies of that special place had a more profound effect on us then we realized. I cancelled five fully booked healing workshops that I was supposed to teach and withdrew into myself. Ultimately it also resulted in my divorce from my second wife, Carina.

At the time, I did not know that my divorce would lead to another step in the direction of the thirteen original skulls. The trip to Mexico had renewed my fascination with the story of the thirteen crystal skulls. Do they really exist? Who made them, or who brought them to the Earth? Where are they?

Searching for the Thirteen Portals

Looking back to the years 1997 to 1998, there was one main theme in my life: experiencing the energies of the thirteen original crystal skulls. I worked with several psychic women and meditated a lot. After a while, I no longer had any doubt that the fundamental principle of "original skulls" was true. When something feels right, it feels right in my whole being. The basic principle of the existence of original crystal skulls that contained information felt right. It also felt right that the number of these crystal skulls had something to do with the number thirteen, although I knew there was more to it than a simple: "There are thirteen original crystal skulls." At the same time, I had the feeling that once I knew more about the principle of thirteen original crystal skulls, other information would follow.

In one of my meditations, I felt that the best approach would be to feel into *portals*, doorways into other realms or dimensions through which these original crystal skulls may have come to Earth. I believed that once I had established the location of these portals, I would begin to have a deeper understanding of these skulls and may even be able to experience their energies.

It has been an interesting journey. Through a combination of meditation and virtual map dowsing—virtual dowsing is dowsing without any instruments; the instrument is you, yourself—over time thirteen places were found. I believe these are the portals through which the original crystal skulls came to Earth. My findings were confirmed by a number of psychics, who either felt similar things or could have picked up what I believed. Nonetheless, it was helpful, especially because I still had my own difficulties in believing in what I had found. For that reason, I did not share this information with people other than close friends and a year later with Jeanne, my wife-to-be. Actually, it wasn't until 2006 before it felt right to share this information on a larger scale—after many years of endless checking, testing and meditations, first with Jeanne and later with the weekly crystal skull meditation group in our house and then even later with larger audiences.

Initially, I only had a list of names of locations, which I finally put on a map [see Fig. 35]. During this period, I was also working with the

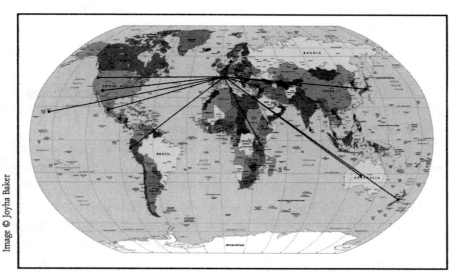

Image © Joyha Baker

Fig. 35. The location of the thirteen crystal skull portals and the lines that connect the twelve portals with the central one (the thirteenth).

Photo © Jaap van Etten

Fig. 36. Symbol of the central portal at Rennes-le-Château that I made from copper wire.

five Platonic solids. Within each Platonic solid, all sides, all faces and all angles are the same. What differs is how many sides, faces and angles a solid has and what the form of the face is.

I made the five Platonic solids from copper wire, which I soldered together. Working with the portals and making Platonic solids simultaneously obviously did something with me. I could wake up in the middle of the night and see a symbol, and then hear that I needed to make it. My tendency was to not remember the next morning. However, the images came back, and one night I woke up simply knowing that these symbols had something to do with the thirteen portals. Finally I gave in and started to make notes during the night and during meditations. This led to the creation of thirteen symbols, which

I made from copper wire [see Fig. 36]. Each represents the energy signature of one of the portals.

I also looked into the possible star systems that these portals are connected with. Connecting with these star systems was very challenging for me. I had insufficient knowledge about the different star systems and did not know how I could connect with something I knew little about. Nonetheless, there seemed to be a guiding force helping me to find the names. This guiding force also helped me to feel the truth of the found connections. All the information on the portals that was collected over this time is summarized in Table 6.

Visiting the Portal Locations

Over time I have visited several of the portal locations. The place in Mexico that my friends and I were guided to for our Atlantis adventure is one of these portals. Another place I have visited many times is the so-called Viking borough in Fyrkat, Denmark. I had never associated this place with crystal skulls. However, I and several people I knew associated Fyrkat with extraterrestrials, which was also the experience of several sensitive people I brought to this place. A third place I had visited is the center of a large five-pointed star in the landscape of southern France, of which Rennes-le-Château is a part. This center is called Coste de Laval and is the location of the portal of the thirteenth skull, the central skull.

It seemed that as soon as I had made the symbols and was able to connect deeper with the thirteen portals, a phase was completed. My attention shifted back again to the study of Earth energies and I felt a strong impulse to revisit Sedona. I wanted to do two things in Sedona: I wanted to study the vortexes, which at that time seemed to be something unique to Sedona, and I also wanted to look for the portal of one of the thirteen original skulls, which I felt was located in the Sedona area.

On June 16, 1998, I arrived in Sedona. Two things happened, although I didn't know that both would be part of the continuation

Location	Coordinates	Star System	Keyword	Symbol
Denmark, Hobro, Fyrkat	56°38′ N 09°48′ E	Pleiades	Healing	
Japan, Mount Fuji	35°21′ N 138°46′ E	Cassiopeia	Understanding	
China, Himalayas, Kunlunshan Area	37°00′ N 76°38′ E	Andromeda	Love	
Turkey, Adana Province, Taurus Mountains, Near Pozanti	37°37′ N 35°03′ E	Alpha Centauri	Integration	
New Zealand, Mount Cook	43°37′ S 170°10′ E	Arcturus	Teaching	
Australia, Ayers Rock	25°22′ S 131°06′ E	Orion	Duality/Oneness	
Tanzania, Mount Kilimanjaro	02°58′ S 37°25′ E	Cygnus	Grace	

Location	Coordinates	Star System	Keyword	Symbol
Peru, Chiclayo, Sacred Laguna, Near Huncabamba	05°10′ S 79°30′ W	Ursa Major (Big Dipper)	Insight	*(symbol)*
Mexico, Sierra Madras, San Patricio	22°75′ N 104°48′ W	Zeta Reticuli	Change	*(symbol)*
U.S.A., Maui, Hawaii, Haleakala Crater	20°44′ N 156°07′ W	Dragon	Transmutation	*(symbol)*
U.S.A., Sedona, Arizona	34°54′ N 111°48′ W	Sirius	Knowledge	*(symbol)*
U.S.A., Mount Shasta, California	41°27′ N 122°11′ W	Taurus	Transformation	*(symbol)*
France, Rennes-le-Château, Coste de Laval	42°53′ N 02°12′ E	Central Skull	Union	*(symbol)*

Table 6. Summary of the portal locations associated with the original skulls and the star systems they are connected to. Included here are the keywords and symbols that represent each portal's energy signature.

of my crystal skull journey. I bought my third crystal skull in a shop in Sedona (a three-inch clear quartz crystal skull) and I met Jeanne. We fell in love, I moved to Sedona and we got married at the end of that year.

My relationship with Jeanne not only changed my life in a general way but it also gave me a very strong impulse to deepen my connection with crystal skulls. Jeanne immediately loved the crystal skulls. As a gemstone and diamond therapist, she was very connected with crystals, and for her it was easy to flow into a deep connection with crystal skulls. Soon our crystal skull family expanded to the 120 we now own. We started to meditate with crystal skulls more than I had ever done alone, and we expanded our knowledge by sharing our experiences. Part of that was the continuation of connecting with and experiencing the energies of the portals.

In the very beginning of our relationship, we found the portal in Sedona. It was located near a place that many people enjoy hiking to, called Devil's Bridge. This place was described by Nicholas Mann as the center of a hexagram that he found in the Sedona landscape [see Plate 17].[8]

On our honeymoon, we went to the coast of California and to Mount Shasta. Here we found another portal that belonged to the group of thirteen. It was still challenging to feel the energies connected to the portals. From the ones that I had experienced so far, the strongest for me was the one in Mexico. I was not overly impressed by the energies of the portal I found in Sedona. The same was true for the one on Mount Shasta. Were my expectations too high?

In 1999, Jeanne and I visited Maui. Here we searched for yet another portal. We found it in the Haleakala Crater, close to the visitor's center. This was a very powerful place, but the energy was related to the different powerful Earth energy vortexes in the area and not so much to the portal. So far none of the portals, with the exception of the one in Mexico, gave me the feeling of a deep connection with crystal skulls.

Bryan de Flores' Thirteen Crystal Skull Accelerator Images

After our trip to Maui came a period with very limited focus on the portals. Almost all our energy was focused on a deeper understanding of the polyhedral fields of the crystal skulls. That changed in January 2002, when Jeanne and I attended a lecture/workshop of Bryan de Flores.[9] Bryan had experienced a dramatic shift in consciousness in December 1996, and as a consequence, he became an artist and started to create what he calls "images from the Divine Blueprint."

These extraordinary multidimensional images are accelerators to prepare humankind for the shift in consciousness that so many people believe is imminent. These images include thirteen accelerators with crystal skull images, each of which has a name connected with a civilization. At the moment he created the images, Bryan did not know anything about crystal skulls; he actually had not seen a crystal skull until after he had made them. During the lecture we attended, he showed the thirteen crystal skull accelerators, and the participants were guided into meditation to experience more deeply the energy of these accelerators. Jeanne and I were impressed, and we bought the set of thirteen crystal skull accelerators. These thirteen images started the next phase in studying the thirteen original crystal skulls.

In getting images of the thirteen crystal skulls without knowing anything about them, Bryan may have tapped into either the collective (un)consciousness or into the akashic records. Wherever his information and inspiration came from, I felt that it had something to do with the original crystal skulls. Bryan created accelerators, images that had certain energies. The question arose whether the energy of the crystal skull accelerators resonated in one way or another with the thirteen portals and the thirteen symbols I had made. I felt very strongly that this was the case. Could it be that each crystal skull has an energy signature that makes it resonate with one of the thirteen groups?

By that time, Jeanne and I were caretakers of quite a number of crystal skulls. We wondered many times why we felt guided to collect so many different skulls. We never got the answer but trusted that it was the right thing to do. Now I had the answer. In order to play with the energies and the possibility that there are thirteen energy groups, we needed to have enough crystal skulls to work with. Preferably we needed to have examples of each of the thirteen groups.

The process of feeling the essence of each of the thirteen groups and then feeling to which group each individual crystal skull belonged turned out to be more challenging than I had anticipated. It took us quite some time to get an understanding about the essence of these thirteen energy groups, and it took even longer to assign each crystal skull to one of the thirteen groups. Some of the crystal skulls have an energy that is strongly in alignment with the energy of one of the groups, so the energy is easily recognizable. Other crystal skulls have an energy that makes it less easy to recognize to which group they belong.

Soon we understood that the degree of activation also plays a role. The more a skull is activated, the easier it is to recognize the specific group signature. We also discovered that some crystal skulls have an energy that seems to be more diffuse, so it becomes more difficult to assign this crystal skull to a certain group. In such a case, we assigned the crystal skull to the group that felt closest. Once the crystal skull was placed in the group and we worked with it for a while, it became integrated into that group. Sometimes a crystal skull was assigned to a group, but then months later we came to the conclusion that it had been assigned to the wrong group. This process taught us a lot about crystal skulls and their energies. After we completed the process in 2003, we worked intensely with the energies of the thirteen groups.

Working with Portal Groups

After 2004 we no longer felt guided to continue working with the crystal skull accelerators of Bryan de Flores. In that period, our focus was on things other than the thirteen skulls. We were working again mainly with the process of activation and with PHFs. We did visit the portal in Sedona a number of times, but the focus on portals and crystal skulls seemed to diminish for that period of time [see Plate 18].

In 2005 we started organizing monthly crystal skull meditations in our house. This soon grew into a bimonthly meditation, and by the beginning of 2006, it became a weekly crystal skull meditation. With the support of the participants, we made it into a playground, creating many different energy fields supported by the crystal skulls. During that time, I was invited to give a lecture and workshop during a crystal skull conference in Holland, organized by Joshua Shapiro, which brought up a serious question for me: Did I want to share the information I had gathered about the portals and their connections to the star systems and to the thirteen crystal skulls? When I brought this query into the meditation group, everybody encouraged me to do so.

All the crystal skulls we had were in the large room that we used for the meditations. They were there constantly, but the configuration in which the crystal skulls were placed fluctuated. Jeanne changed the placement depending on the field she wanted to create, which in turn depended upon the focus of the meditation of that evening. At some point we organized the crystal skulls into thirteen groups based on their connection with the thirteen portals.

This time we did not include the accelerators of Bryan de Flores— they have their own unique function as accelerators, but their energies are not completely in alignment with what we were doing. The accelerators had fulfilled a function that led to a deeper connection with and a greater sensitivity for the energies of the crystal skulls in general and the thirteen portals and their characteristic energy qualities in particular, and I felt deep gratitude for that. However, it was time to continue on without them. Instead of the accelerators, we now placed the thirteen symbols I had made almost ten years earlier in the center of each of the thirteen groups [see Plate 20].

During the meditations, we invited the participants to choose one of the groups and to work only with the crystal skulls from the group they had chosen. Some participants worked with some of the crystal skulls of the group they had chosen; others felt that they needed to hold all of them. Jeanne introduced another way of working with a portal group. She placed the crystal skulls of a group around her and sat herself in the center. In that way, she created a situation in which she *was* the portal or doorway, open to receive whatever she could. Her example was soon followed by other participants.

After a couple of meditations, we realized that the energy of each of the portal groups became stronger. We changed the placement of the groups and located them in the circle relative to their respective portals' actual geographical location in the world, which increased the energy again. Finally, based on our experiences and those of the participants, we attributed a keyword to each of the groups [see Table 6]. This changed the essence of many of the meditations. Initially people shared experiences that were clearly based on their experiences with individual skulls. After a while, however, the sharing changed. The experiences were still based on the connection with individual skulls, but more often people would start sharing experiences that were based on the essence of the energies of the portal groups. Every meditation evening brought a large variety of wonderful experiences.

The Satellite Portals

There was one final discovery that completed this phase of the connections with and understanding of the portal energies and groups. Using the RFI™ method (see chapter 5), I wanted to measure Sam when he was placed in the center of the portal in Sedona. Unfortunately, the results did not help me gain any insights leading to a deeper understanding of the interaction of a crystal skull and the energies of the portal. Whatever the effects were, it was not measurable in the range from 1 MHz to 3 GHz.

In an earlier measurement, done without Sam at the same location, I had already discovered that when I measure the frequencies in the center of the portal at different heights, the frequency changes. Starting at ground level, the measured frequencies increased as they were taken at increasing heights. A couple of feet away from the center, this effect was much weaker. However, there were three areas where I noticed a similar phenomenon as in the center of the portal. Here the frequencies of the measured energies also increased when I measured at increasing heights above ground level.

One of these places was where I had located an energy line that connected the portal in Sedona with the central portal near Rennes-le-Château. It is possible to dowse these connecting lines, and the measurements in megahertz supported the results obtained with dowsing. The RFI™ measurements, however, suggested a second and third line. When I followed the second line, I connected to another smaller portal on a hill in front of Chimney Rock, about 1.8 miles south of the main portal [see Plate 19]. The Sedona portal had some kind of a satellite! Further research showed that the third line went to a place in Secret Canyon, about 2.8 miles north of the main portal. This means there are two secondary portals connected with the Sedona portal! Sitting on a secondary portal gives a similar feeling as the main portal—that each portal has its own crystal skull. The three crystal skulls connected with the three portals work together in a way that so far I have not been able to comprehend.

The question immediately arises: How many of these satellite portals exist? Does each portal have two additional portals? From the information I have gleaned through meditation, the answer is yes. Each of the main portals has two additional portals, which brings the total number of secondary portals to twenty-four and the total number of original skulls to thirty-six, with the addition of a central skull. I had come across the number thirty-six before in *Mysteries of the Crystal Skulls Revealed*. Sandra Bowen shared this during an interview with Joshua Shapiro and Jeff Cohen; the information was channeled. She was asked whether there were other crystal skulls on Earth like the Mitchell-Hedges Skull and the rose quartz skull Nick Nocerino had once seen: crystal skulls that are about human size and have a detachable jaw. Her answer was: "There are thirty six that are of different colors. They are clear, pure, radiant and placed all over the world in triads or groups of three."[10] It is interesting that I had found through dowsing and RFI™ measurement similar numbers. The only difference is that she does not mention the central crystal skull. I see each "triad" as one energy system, which means that we fundamentally still talk about twelve energy groups with a thirteenth crystal skull that brings this group of skulls into one energy field, one field of information.

In the same interview, they asked Sandra Bowen whether there is a focal point where the energy of the thirty-six crystal skulls merges together. Her answer was that the culmination of their combined energy meets in a pyramid in the etheric plane over Tibet. She believes that for various reasons this focal point will eventually move to the Four Corners area in the southwestern part of the United States.[11] Whether there is any truth to this is something that everybody needs to feel for themselves. I feel that the original focus point was in Atlantis. After the destruction of Atlantis, the survivors spread in different directions. One of the places they went to was the southern part of France, before most of the people moved on to Egypt. While staying in the South of France, the point near Rennes-le-Château was established. In my opinion, this is currently the focal point.

Reactivating the Portals

During my visits to the Sedona portal, a question came up. With exception of the portal in Mexico, why do I not feel powerful energy while I am at one of the portals? With my connection to the crystal skulls, I expected more of a connection with such a portal. The answer turned out to be very simple: These portals are not very active. Actually, the whole system of portals and supporting portals has a very low activity level. Either the portals were consciously deactivated, or the fact that people have lost their ability to connect with them has led to a deactivation. Whatever the case, I felt it was important to activate these portals again. Only when we have the ability to activate and connect with the portals will we be able to connect with the original skulls in their fullness and access the information that is connected with them.

At this moment (mid-2007), the Sedona portal is at 49 percent of its maximum activation. The Mexico portal is more active (59 percent of its optimum) and it had this level of activation when I went to it in 1996. I do not understand why this portal has this high level of activation compared to all the other portals in this system.

Besides the Mexico portal, the Sedona portal is for now the most active portal, mainly because it is also the center of the six-pointed star in the Sedona landscape. In the past few years (2004–2006), a number of activation ceremonies have taken place that have undoubtedly had an effect on the portal itself.[12] Noneheless, the activation is still rather limited, and this is even more true for the other portals. In other words, there is a lot of work ahead of us.

I do believe that we can do those activations from the comfort of our house. Whatever skull we have, it is connected to one of the portals. After activating your crystal skull, in meditation you can set as an intent that you want to activate the portal your skull is connected with. I am sure that when enough people do this, the portals will be activated again. I believe this will allow the information that is connected with the original skulls to become available. The more this information and these energies become available, the more it will support the evolution of our human consciousness.

CHAPTER 9

Other Stories of the Original Thirteen Skulls

I have shared with you my discoveries about the legend of the thirteen skulls. I also have mentioned that my ideas have similarities to those of Sandra Bowen. It may be interesting to see what other people and traditions say about this legend.

Many people who work with crystal skulls have heard the story that Nick Nocerino is the one who brought the story of the thirteen crystal skulls into the world. There is no doubt that Nocerino believes in the story.[1] Yet as we have already seen, this story or legend is older than the vision of Nick Nocerino. It is a story that has been told many times by different Native American elders as part of their tradition.

The Teachings of Harley Swiftdeer

The story I read in Kenneth Meadow's book about the thirteen crystal skulls was shared again in *The Mystery of the Crystal Skulls*, where Morton and Thomas interview Harley Swiftdeer. Here he presents himself not as a Cherokee medicine man but as "the heyokah or war chief of the Twisted Hairs Society's council of elders," and he tells the story of the singing skulls and the Ark of Osiriaconwiya.[2] I would like to share some of his teachings.

The Twisted Hairs Society includes members from over four hundred different tribes from North, South and Central America. This means this story has a lot of weight, for it represents the essence of the Native American belief structure on this subject. According to his story, in the beginning there were twelve worlds with human life. These planets were also called the sacred twelve planets, or the Grandmothers. One of them was Earth, which according to Harley was called the planet of the children because it was the least evolved. To help the planet of the children, each planet decided to create a container for the sum total of all of their knowledge. These containers are the crystal skulls—each not just *a* crystal skull, but a flawless, perfect crystal skull with a detachable jaw. They were referred to as the singing skulls.[3]

The entire configuration of twelve crystal skulls was known as the Ark of Osiriaconwiya. The elders brought the Ark to the Earth and began to work with the people and teach them. According to Harley Swiftdeer, they helped the people of Earth to build four civilizations: Lemuria, Mu, Mieyhun and Atlantis. They used the knowledge of the crystal skulls to begin the great mystery schools, the arcane wisdom schools and the secret medicine societies. Through them they spread the information.[4]

According to Swiftdeer, the information—does he mean the crystal skulls?—arrived approximately 750,000 years ago, and it began to disseminate on Grandmother Earth around 250,000 to 300,000 years ago. It is not clear where in time he places the four civilizations that the elders helped to build. Swiftdeer tells us that the twelve crystal skulls were kept inside a pyramid in a circle with a central skull that was larger than the others. The thirteenth skull represented the collective consciousness of the world.[5]

Swiftdeer then jumps ahead in time, making the following statement: "The traveling people that first brought the Ark of the singing skulls came to be known as the 'Olmec,' then it migrated up and was taken over in legacy by the Mayans and then by the Aztecs. This knowledge today is still held by the Twisted Hair."[6] According to Swiftdeer, the Ark was in Teotihuacán when the Spanish army came, led by Cortés. Just before the Spaniards arrived, the "jaguar priests and eagle warriors" took the skulls and fled. Basically, they scattered over the Earth, which was the first time these skulls had separated since they came to Earth. It is believed that it is not yet the right time for them to reunite.[7]

Swiftdeer mentions that many other crystal skulls were made, but they did not have a detachable lower jaw. They were therefore called the "talking" skulls, to separate them from the "singing" skulls.[8]

If I understand the story correctly, one of the thirteen skulls was a crystal skull that contained the sum of all knowledge of the Earth. This is confusing, because the containers (crystal skulls) were made to help the Earth. Given the state of consciousness the Earth was in, who would have been able to create the crystal skull containing the sum of all knowledge of the Earth?

Morton and Thomas were not sure either whether the information Swiftdeer gave was correct. Not all his information fit with other information they had gathered. After all, a heyokah, the trickster, can easily put you into a state of confusion.

OɣheR Naɣive SɣoRies

Another Native American who has shared information in Morton and Thomas' book is Don Alejandro Cirilo Perez Oxlaj.[9] He is a high priest of the Quiche Mayan Council of Elders, which represents twenty-one different Mayan regions. According to him, there are more than thirteen crystal skulls. The Mayans originally had thirteen, but other crystal skulls were left with other indigenous peoples around the world. According to the original teachings passed down through the council, there were originally fifty-two crystal skulls in various sacred centers around the world, including many with other Native American tribes and even some in Tibet and with the Aborigines of Australia.[10]

Don Alejandro says that the number fifty-two, like the number thirteen, is very sacred to the Mayan people. He adds that the crystal skulls have helped the indigenous people to keep their traditions and cultures alive through some very difficult times in the past and continue to do so today. For the Council, the crystal skulls are the mothers and fathers of science and of wisdom. He adds to that: "All of the knowledge and wisdom of the entire world, and the universe, is contained in those crystal skulls."[11]

Morton and Thomas also extensively interviewed Leon Secatero, the spiritual leader of the Canoncito Indians in New Mexico—part of the Navajo tribe.[12] Secatero admits they have a crystal skull that they keep hidden. They consider it to be too sacred to allow others to come close to it; only the shaman who looks after the skull knows where it is. To the Spaniards, the Canoncito Indians were known as the "skull people" because the land they lived on had the shape of a skull. According to Secatero, the original crystal skulls were made by the Holy Ones. He believes they are part of a crystal matrix that links the people of Earth with the rest of the universe. Secatero says that later humans also began to make crystal skulls. These skulls have been crafted using human hair, because human hair is sacred. Hairs are like the antennae to the soul.[13]

According to Secatero, the Navajo understanding is that the crystal skulls made by the Holy Ones are like a prototype for the human species. It is like a blueprint, a template, a matrix. He says they are like a field that contains the information that is needed to give form to a species. Such fields exist for each species of animal and also the human.[14] This idea is interesting and refers to what Rupert Sheldrake calls morphogenetic fields (Sheldrake proposed the idea of a field containing the blueprint for each species).[15]

It is understandable why the Navajos have such a reference for crystal skulls. They believe that as long as the crystal skulls exist, we will exist. The crystal skulls will change with us when we human beings change. They believe that every human being is connected to the crystal skulls. The skulls emit a sound that can only be heard with the inner ear, and for that reason, they are called the singing skulls. The wisdom of the crystal skulls becomes available when you open yourself to this mystery and let the sound come in.[16]

Another person Morton and Thomas interviewed was Jamie Sams.[17] Sams also shares that it was extraterrestrials that brought the crystal skulls to the Earth. They came from the sky: from the Pleiades, from Orion, from Sirius. They were looking for a new home and brought the crystal skulls as gifts with them. These crystal skulls contain all the knowledge of these people from the other planets; everything about these people was stored in those skulls.[18]

According to Sams, the crystal skulls also had another function: They were the template for a new species. She believes the Neanderthals stored information about their evolution in the brain, and consequently the brain became larger during the evolutionary process. This created problems with birth. The crystal skulls formed the matrix of a species that stored evolutionary information in their DNA. She shares that the DNA of the Neanderthals and that of the extraterrestrials were mixed to create Homo sapiens. The crystal skulls contain the blueprint for this new species.[19]

Personal Visions and Experiences

Although the information about the original or singing or thirteen crystal skulls shared by the different Native American people comes from certain individuals, it is based on legends and stories that have been passed on from generation to generation for a long time. That gives these stories a certain value. In addition to the stories of the Native people, many people who work with crystal skulls have personal visions and experiences about the original crystal skulls. In a time that more people feel attracted to crystal skulls, the number of these visions has increased. Searching the Internet and talking with people during crystal skull gatherings gives many stories, each having its value as a personal experience. Most of these stories are based on the number twelve with a central thirteenth crystal skull. I would like to mention a few of these visions, especially those that are documented and are relevant for the understanding of the story of the thirteen original crystal skulls.

Some interesting stories and information are documented in the book *Mysteries of the Crystal Skulls Revealed*. The first one is a story shared by Michael Kant, based on his channeling.[20] He believes there are thirteen crystal skulls (original crystal skulls) that are under the Potala in Tibet. These crystal skulls are placed in a circle in such a way that they form two Stars of David, and the thirteenth is in the center. He believes the thirteen crystal skulls are symbolic of the thirteen Atlantean healing temples, the thirteen Inner Earth tribes, the fifty-two-year sacred calendar of the Mayans and so on.[21]

According to Kant, the crystal skull and other examples of crystal and light technologies were brought to Earth by various galactic races, such as that of the Pleiadians during the time of Atlantis. These races formed the thirteen tribes of the Inner Earth.[22] He sees the origin of the Mitchell-Hedges Skull in one of the thirteen healing temples in Atlantis, which he says is located in the Bimini area. As discussed in chapter 7, he believes that the Mitchell-Hedges Skull comes from a female priest-ess who was killed during one of the last earthquakes on Atlantis. Her skull was transformed into crystal through the crystal science of mor-phocrystallic transformation.[23]

Kant mentions that there are several techniques that were used in the past to create crystal skulls (he is not talking about the later technique of carving a crystal). The technique that created the singing—he calls them "original"—crystal skulls (now under the Potala in Tibet) was morphocrystallic generation. This process uses an etheric matrix form, or what the creators seem to call "thought crystal." According to Kant, this technique was used by other extraterrestrial races and they actually created whole crystal skeletons. This is a way to create high frequency crystal skulls.[24]

As I mentioned, according to Kant, the Mitchell-Hedges Skull was cre-ated through morphocrystallic transformation. That means that an actual form, the matrix—in this case, the skull of a priestess—was already there and through thought was transformed into quartz crystal. I feel that the theory on morphocrystallic generation and morphocrystallic transformation is correct. I was aware of these processes in the beginning of the 1990s when I was studying crystals and the factors influencing the growth of crystals. Neither the people I worked with nor I gave a name to the process. Kant's terms clearly describe the process, and for that reason, I have adopted his terminology. Morphocrystallic generation and morphocrystallic transformation both create crystals and crystal skulls with high frequencies that are given form by six extra polyhedral fields as described in chapter 5.

In the same book, Sandra Bowen mentions information similar to that of Kant. She connected with the Mitchell-Hedges Skull and also felt that it was the skull of a priestess from Atlantis.[25] It is interesting that Frank Dorland in his book *Holy Ice* summarizes research done on the Mitchell-Hedges Skull, which shows that the crystal skull is a copy of a real skull of a female of the Mongoloid race aged between twenty-five and twenty-nine years.[26]

In a regression, Sandra Bowen connected with a past life in which she worked with the thirteen crystal skulls under the Potala in Tibet. She sees the crystal skulls in Tibet as an etheric form, whereas the Mitchell-Hedges crystal skull is more of an Earth representative. Sandra Bowen also mentions that the crystal skulls relate to each of the thirteen Inner Earth tribes.[27]

Spoon Bending and the Morphocrystallic Processes

Processes like morphocrystallic generation and morphocrystallic transformation seem far-fetched. Are there any indications that such processes could have existed? I believe so. There is a phenomenon that can give us an indication how these processes may work—this phenomenon is called spoon bending.

Spoon bending has popularity as a spectacular method to prove and train the power of the mind. Out of curiosity, I attended a workshop in Holland facilitated by an American woman. During the preparation, all eighty participants were saying to the spoon or fork they had in their hand, "Bend, bend, bend," many times. We held the utensil between the thumb and index finger of both hands and put a very light pressure at both ends as if we wanted to bend it. The idea was not to force but to wait until we could feel that the spoon became soft somewhere. Another method was to rub the spoon at a certain place until we felt a change occurring.

As soon as we felt that a part of the spoon became soft, it could be bent effortlessly in any direction. I will never forget when that moment came. With only slight pressure, it was easy to feel how suddenly a part of the spoon I held shifted its consistency and I could bend it without any effort. It was an exhilarating feeling! The bending became almost secondary; the feeling was all that seemed to matter to me. A photo was taken of that moment and it appeared in a few magazines. My happy moment was captured for many to see!

At the time, I believed it was the power of the mind that did it. Now I am aware that there is more to it than only mind power. I believe that spoon bending can help us understand the principle behind the morphocrystallic sciences.

I would like to repeat a statement I made earlier: Everything is energy. What we call physical form—i.e. something we can see and touch—is in reality an energy that has a certain frequency. What we see as visible is an energy field that has a frequency our eyes are able to perceive and we can touch it. Our brain has learned that what we feel and see as solid is different from what we call energy.

What we call energy cannot generally be perceived with our five physical senses. However, science tells us that what we perceive as solid is more than 95 percent empty space. The atoms that create the molecules that give the shape of the object consist of a nucleus and electrons. The electrons swarm around the nucleus in clouds, indicating the most likely place where we can find them, and they create the energy fields around a nucleus, which creates the "space." The movements of the electrons indicate the energetic state of the atom. In other words, we are looking at an energy field that has such a frequency that it absorbs and reflects light in a way where we perceive a certain form with certain colors.

If we believe that the spoon is a solid form that is unchangeable under normal circumstances, it will be exactly that for us: something that cannot be changed. However, we can also believe that the spoon is an energy form. Because all energy can be changed through intent, it is possible to change a spoon. One way is to change it into a bent spoon. When all participants were saying, "Bend, bend, bend," like a mantra, they created a collective field that was holding the belief that it is possible to bend a spoon. People who could resonate with this belief were able to bend the spoon; participants who could not believe this is possible could not do it. The fact that some people did bend a spoon strengthened the energy field of the "believers," and eventually more people were able to actually bend their spoons.

Later, when I did the spoon bending by myself, it was more difficult to get results. Sometimes I was successful, and sometimes my doubts were too strong to succeed. The process of spoon bending is a process of belief, trust and training. Initially I believed it was easier to bend a thin spoon than a thick spoon, but I learned that the thickness of the material does not really matter unless I choose to believe that it does.

In essence, the morphocrystallic processes work in the same way. It is a matter of clear intent and a belief that we can change or create what we want. Granted, the morphocrystallic processes are more complex. When we bend a spoon, we work with molecules of the same type. We even use the same basic form, although we twist the form so it looks different. We change the vibration of the molecules to allow them to be malleable into the form from our imagination. I have even twisted the spoon around a couple of times and I have seen even more elaborate results.

In the process of morphocrystallic transformation, we do not change the form (matrix). In that process, we change the energy in such a way that we create a different molecular structure. We transform bone into crystal, much like the alchemists of olden times who changed lead into gold. In the process of morphocrystallic generation, we initially do not have a form (matrix). The first step in the process is to create such a matrix (thought form), which is then used to create a crystal or a crystal skull. This is the most advanced technique.

In our time, we do not have the awareness or the training to use the morphocrystallic processes. I believe we lost this skill a long time ago. Most likely, the overall vibration most of us function on does not even allow us to use these processes. However, my experiences with bending spoons show me that our abilities to change energy fields that create form are more developed than we may think. I would not be surprised if one day somebody demonstrates that morphocrystallic processes are again within our reach. Until that time, we have the choice to either accept or reject the possibility that morphocrystallic processes exist.

I have chosen to accept the existence of these processes. Every time I connect with the Mitchell-Hedges Skull, I feel I am tapping into that potential. While bending my spoons, I had a strong sensing of these possibilities we all have. Are you the one who will show us how to use the processes of morphocrystallic generation and/or morphocrystallic transformation?

CHAPTER 10

The Number 12 + 1

The general consensus seems to be that there are thirteen original skulls. When people mention that there are more than thirteen crystal skulls, they almost always mention numbers that are multiples of twelve or thirteen, such as thirty-six or fifty-two.

The number thirteen is sacred for the Mayans. Since many skulls have been found in the Mayan area, many people associate the number thirteen with Mayan traditions and predictions. However, the number 12 + 1 is common in many traditions and religions. There are so many examples that it is beyond the scope of this book to cover this subject, so I will only mention a few: There are twelve hours on a clock, twelve months in a year, twelve signs of the zodiac, and Jesus had twelve disciples.

Christianity and the Numbers Twelve and Thirteen

It is interesting to summarize a text from Revelation, chapter 21 about the Heavenly City, the City of God. The city has twelve gates with the names of the twelve tribes on them. Twelve angels stand at the gates, the walls have twelve foundations garnished with twelve precious stones, and in them are the names of the twelve apostles. The city is twelve thousand furlongs square, and the twelve gates have twelve pearls. The number twelve is used here symbolically of God's perfect government. Twelve is mentioned nine times here. Note that the length, breadth and height are all equal, all twelve thousand furlongs. If we count this as three measures of twelve rather than just one, then the number twelve is mentioned twelve times in this passage of twelve verses.

In that sense, it is interesting to see what the thinking in Christianity is about the number thirteen. If twelve is the perfect government of God, the addition of one will lead to less than perfect. There are many examples that indicate that thirteen actually refers to destruction. So thirteen became a number of ill-fate. How can a number in one tradition be sacred and in another tradition be a number of bad omen? Is there a reason why Christianity chose to focus on the number twelve as the number of disciples Jesus had instead of mentioning Jesus and his twelve disciples as a group of thirteen?

Sacred Geometry and the Platonic Solids

To understand the numbers twelve and thirteen, we need to first look at sacred geometry and specifically at the Platonic solids. Platonic solids are polyhedral, which means they have many faces. These polyhedral forms are only called Platonic solids when all the faces are equal, with equal sides and equal angles always meeting at the sides. There are five such forms, also called regular polyhedrals: the tetrahedron, the cube (hexahedron), the octahedron, the dodecahedron and the icosahedron.[1] For our exploration of the numbers twelve and thirteen, we will focus on one of the five Platonic solids called the dodecahedron. This geometric shape has twelve faces, which are all identical pentagons. Each pentagon has five equal sides [see Figs. 37 and 38].

Each Platonic solid is associated with one of the elements: the tetrahedron with fire, the octahedron with air, the icosahedron with water and the cube with earth. Of the fifth, the dodecahedron, Plato said: ". . . God used it for arranging the constellations on the whole heaven." In general, it is said that Plato associated the dodecahedron with the universe.

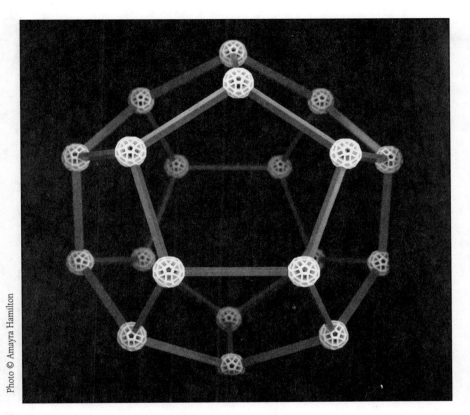

Fig. 37. An example of a dodecahedron.

Plato's thought turns out to have more validity than people used to think. In an article in the scientific magazine *Nature*, cosmologists in France and the U.S. suggest that space could be finite and shaped like a dodecahedron. They claim that a universe with the same shape as the twelve-sided polygon can explain measurements of the cosmic microwave background—the radiation left over from the big bang—that spaces with a more mundane shape cannot. Actually they predict that the model consisting of twelve curved pentagons joined together in a sphere agrees most with their observations.[2]

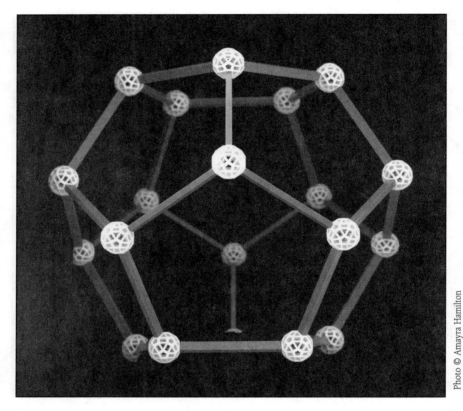

Photo © Amayra Hamilton

Fig. 38. Another view of the dodecahedron.

This implies much: There is an increasing acceptance that we live in a holographic universe.[3] Based on the holographic principles, it is likely that many systems will have a relationship to this fundamental form of the universe: the dodecahedron. This may explain why the number twelve comes back so often in systems that form a functional and informational unit. In that sense, it is not surprising that also the original crystal skulls, which are believed to be a complete system of information, will be based on the same principle—will be based on the number twelve.

The Function of the Thirteenth Element

What remains is the question: What is the function of the thirteenth element? In my opinion, the thirteenth element is always the one that brings the twelve principles or aspects into oneness, into one functional whole. That functional whole is more than the sum of the twelve aspects. It brings the information of all twelve aspects onto a new level of knowledge, insight and consciousness. It is the transcending principle. Once we are able to connect to the thirteenth element, we expand into something new.

That is why the number thirteen is sacred, because the thirteenth element helps us to transcend this reality into something new. Jesus represents this, and we call what he represents the Christ consciousness, which is the consciousness that is beyond the one we live in at the moment. The twelve disciples represent our current consciousness. It seems that the number thirteen is not a number of bad luck; rather, it is a sacred number. In that way, the Mayans are right. Understanding the principle of the number thirteen is key for the evolution of our consciousness.

The twelve original crystal skulls all contain information that is very valuable. It can enrich our lives and help us to expand our consciousness. However, these twelve crystal skulls alone will not lead to our next evolutionary step. For that we need the thirteenth skull to transcend the information of the twelve skulls to a new level, creating a shift in consciousness. According to the legend, isn't that what will happen when all thirteen crystal skulls are brought together?

CHAPTER 11

The Legend of the Thirteen Crystal Skulls: An Integrated View

I n this chapter, I give my personal views on the legend of the thirteen crystal skulls and on crystal skulls in general, based on many years of study, meditation, dowsing and interaction with clairvoyant people and others interested in the skulls. Please connect with this view and feel whether you resonate with it as a whole or in part.

Crystal Skulls Were Brought to Earth to Help Humankind

Most of the stories on crystal skulls have in common the belief that there are crystal skulls that have been brought or sent to Earth. These skulls contain information that is special and important for the human race. What exactly that means may vary among different views, but in general it is believed that this information is being given to humankind by a higher consciousness as a tool to support humans in their evolution.

Mostly it is believed that the higher consciousness consists of twelve extraterrestrial civilizations, and I support this belief. I have found that there are twelve portals that function as doorways between Earth and twelve places in the universe. These twelve doorways are connections to higher levels of consciousness. It is interesting that Bashar calls crystal skulls "doorways."[1] When we talk about the original skulls, the question arises whether they are truly physical skulls or whether they are indeed doorways allowing energy and thus information to pass through. Several crystal skull researchers have already mentioned that the original skulls are etheric, or are moving in and out of physical form.

It is my feeling that the original skulls do not exist in physical form on Earth, at least not at this point in time. In my opinion, they are information/consciousness units we can connect with to help us to move into higher levels of consciousness (the shift). Only when we have pulled all aspects of our being together can we access this level of information/consciousness that we call "the thirteen original crystal skulls." The number thirteen reminds us that we can only reach that state of consciousness (oneness) when we can connect to all twelve elements at the same time. Then we become one with the thirteenth or central skull and experience the fullness of all twelve information systems, allowing us to transcend to another level of awareness.

Other Systems of Twelve

This may seem like an extraordinary idea, but there are other systems that function in a similar way. In chapter 6, we looked at the effect of the crystal skull Sam on Earth energies. The lines we looked at form a complex grid system that can be defined as our collective (un)consciousness. There are twelve grid systems that represent twelve levels of our consciousness. If we master all twelve levels and integrate them into one functional whole, we have mastered the level of consciousness that belongs to the reality we live in, which is often called the third-dimensional consciousness. We master this level of consciousness when we are like the thirteenth crystal skull: we bring all twelve systems into one functional whole. Once we are able to do that, we transcend this consciousness into the Christ consciousness.

These two examples show us that all these systems are based on the same principle: that of the Platonic solid, the dodecahedron. All of this is part of sacred geometry. Drunvalo Melchizedek mentions

Photo © Amayra Hamilton

Fig. 39. The Christ consciousness grid: a dodecahedron with icosacaps.

that the Christ consciousness grid—the matrix that holds the Christ consciousness—is based on the dodecahedron with icosahedral caps [see Fig. 39].[2] An icosahedral cap is like a five-sided pyramid with a regular pentagon as its base. The five sides of the icosahedral cap and the five sides of the pentagon are all of equal length [see Fig. 40]. There are twelve sides on a dodecahedron and consequently there are twelve icosahedral caps. Again we find a system that is based on the number twelve.

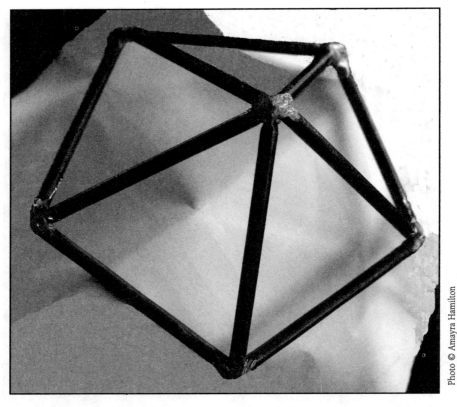

Photo © Amayra Hamilton

Fig. 40. An icosacap: an equilateral pentagon with five equilateral sides on top. All ten sides have the same length. This example was made from copper wire that was soldered together by the author.

It is the human consciousness that has the ability to integrate the twelve levels or aspects of the mentioned systems. This is similar for the crystal skulls. The original crystal skulls form a system of thirteen. Although there are thirty-six portals as described earlier, fundamentally that does not change the principle. There are twelve triads, which means twelve groups of three crystal skulls. They form twelve units, each with a characteristic energy and information that is induced by or connected with an extraterrestrial civilization that has a higher consciousness than currently exists on Earth. Once we are able to fully connect and integrate this system of thirteen original crystal skulls, a new human being will emerge: an enlightened human who has integrated the twelve different aspect of consciousness into oneness.

The Twelve Star Systems

In chapter 8, I gave a list of the twelve types of consciousness that are connected to these twelve portal triads. Is there any support for the names I have mentioned? I have searched for it, but there is not much to be found. Many times people mention that the crystal skulls have something to do with twelve extraterrestrial civilizations, but they do not mention the names or origins of these civilizations. Michael Kant mentions Pleiades, particularly in relation to the Mitchell-Hedges Skull and in relation to the morphocrystallic sciences, and Jamie Sams mentions the Pleiades, Sirius and Orion.[3] But as far as I am aware, there is one other person who has linked the twelve skulls to extraterrestrial civilizations. Kathleen Murray talks about these civilizations in her book *The Divine Spark of Creation: The Crystal Skull Speaks*. According to Murray, there are twelve colors, and each color is connected to a crystal skull, and each of these colored crystal skulls is connected to different star people (extraterrestrial consciousnesses).[4]

In Table 7, I compare the names of the star systems that I feel the original skulls are connected with through the portals, to Kathleen Murray's connections between the star systems and the twelve colored crystal skulls. I am not suggesting that when we use the same names we are necessarily referring to the same energies, but feeling into the colored images that come with her book, there is a high probability. For one skull, she does not give the name of the star people. From the eleven names she mentions, nine names are similar to the names I have found. Sometimes we use different names or focus on a different aspect of the same star system. For example, she mentions Aldebaran, whereas

I mention Taurus. However, Aldebaran is a star in the Taurus constellation. In the second case, she mentions Lyra, which is part of Vega, while she gives a star map that includes both Cygnus and Vega, and I mention Cygnus only.[5]

Therefore, I consider nine cases similar. The ones that are different are indicated in the table by italics. For the two systems that are different, there is another aspect that's similar. Murray mentions that the qualities that belong to the red skull are "Transmutation" and "Transformation," and I have given the quality of "Transmutation" to the Hawaii portal [see Table 6]. For that reason, I have placed them next to each other. The results seem to indicate that Murray and I have tapped into the same source of information on the star systems.

List Author		List Kathleen Murray[6]	
Portal	Star System	Star System	Color Skull
Fyrkat	Pleiades	Pleiades	Aquamarine
Japan	Cassiopeia	Cassiopeia	Silver
Himalayas	Andromeda	Andromeda	Violet
Turkey	Alpha Centauri	Alpha Centauri	Cerise Pink
New Zealand	Arcturus	Arcturus	Golden Skull
Australia	Orion	Orion	Sapphire
Kilimanjaro	Cygnus	Lyra/Cygnus	Electric Blue
Peru	Ursa Major		*Purple*
Mexico	Zeta Reticuli	*Virgo/Spica*	*Pink*
Hawaii	Dragon	*Antares/Scorpio*	*Red*
Sedona	Sirius	Sirius	Green
Mount Shasta	Taurus	Aldebaran/Taurus	Orange

Table 7. List of portals and connected star systems based on the findings of the author and those of Kathleen Murray when she connected with the twelve rays and the connected star system. When the system she mentioned is different from mine, the names are indicated in italics.

A General History of the Crystal Skulls

I do not believe that the original skulls have a physical form. This brings up the question: Which skulls were the first crystal skulls to have a physical form and how many are there? For me, the answer is simple: The first physical crystal skulls are the singing skulls, the crystal skulls that are the size of a human skull and have a detachable jaw. I believe the Mitchell-Hedges Skull is one of these. I also believe that the total number of these crystal skulls is fifty-two. I share the idea of fifty-two crystal skulls with Don Alejandro and Bashar. After the singing skulls, many other crystal skulls were carved. It is in my opinion possible to give a general history of the crystal skulls.

First there were the portal skulls, or original skulls. When the density of our physical reality increased—which means the frequency of the consciousness of humankind decreased—there was a need to create physical skulls. Initially they were created through methods we call morphocrystallic generation and morphocrystallic transformation. In this way, fifty-two singing crystal skulls were created.

The number fifty-two is important, because it is four times thirteen. I feel that at that time in Atlantis, four groups of thirteen crystal skulls were created. "Why four groups?" one may ask. From a historical perspective, all information on Atlantis is based on the story described by the Greek philosopher Plato in two of his dialogues: *Timaeus* and *Critias*. There is no other written record. All current stories about the lost continent of Atlantis are based on the interpretations of these two written dialogues, on interpretations of Native stories and legends from all over the world or on channeled information. The discoveries of sunken cities in the seas along the coasts of many countries feeds the speculations on Atlantis and keeps the legend alive.

Plato describes Poseidon, the holy and royal city of Atlantis, quite extensively. Central in this description by Plato is the geometry of the city, which has had a deep effect on those who connect with the story of Atlantis, because the essence of the layout of the city is a circle with crossing diameters. This is a powerful universal symbol—it divides the circle in four parts. This symbol has several names: it is called the Celtic cross, or even the Atlantean cross.[7] It is also the basic aspect of the medicine wheel, as used in many Native American traditions.

In essence, this symbol represents beliefs about the universe but also about the human being. It represents the four creative powers of the universe, the four elements, the four directions, the four main aspects of a human being (the spiritual, emotional, mental and physical) and the four races, represented by the colors red, yellow, black and white (the colors connected with the four segments or the four directions vary in different traditions).

In my opinion, the four groups of singing crystal skulls represent those four aspects, the four arms of the cross. This symbol can be easily expended into a circle with eight arms (spokes) and that of one with twelve arms. Then we are back to the circle of twelve with the central crystal skull in the middle. In that context, it is interesting that Jamie Sams describes in her book, *The Thirteen Original Clan Mothers*, a medicine wheel as follows: "The Thirteen sisters traveled to the site where the Earth Mother had directed them and found a medicine wheel that had a crystal skull sitting on each of the twelve stones that formed the outer circle, and one sitting on the stone in the center."[8]

The number thirteen can be seen as a spiritual and sacred number. The number four is the number of the Earth, of physical reality. It is for us human beings to bring these two aspects together: the thirteen and the four creating the fifty-two. The number fifty-two truly represents heaven on Earth—the spiritual and the physical into one. It is interesting that Mayan temples have fifty-two steps for human beings to use to go to the temple on top of the pyramid, moving from the physical to the spiritual.

My feeling is that not all four groups of singing crystal skulls survived the destruction of Atlantis. My sensing is that two complete groups did survive, one group is under water and the fourth group was partly destroyed. A total of thirty-one singing crystal skulls were spread over the world after Atlantis disappeared. One group went to Tibet and stayed together as a group for a long time (Sandra Bowen and Michael Kant refer to this group in their interviews in *Mysteries of the Crystal Skulls Revealed*).[9] However, it feels that this group is no longer together and has spread to different locations to keep them out of the hands of the Chinese army. The second group went to Central America but did not stay together. Five more also survived Atlantis from the fourth group and are also somewhere in the Central and South America areas.

When the survivors of Atlantis were spread over the world, the legend of the crystal skulls persisted. The longing to create a new world also induced the longing to use the information that was given to humankind to help them move into a new area, a new world, a new way of living, a new age. They believed they could connect to this information by creating new crystal skulls. But due to the destruction of Atlantis and the continuation of the stepping down in frequency of human consciousness, the knowledge to create crystal skulls through morphocrystallic generation or morphocrystallic transformation was lost. The only way to create them was through carving—using whatever tools they had available and most likely with a lot of patience.

My feeling is that many crystal skulls were made and often—but surely not always—in groups of thirteen. At the moment, these crystal skulls form the group of the fully activated skulls. These crystal skulls are not as homogenous as the group of the singing crystal skulls, for they were made by different civilizations in different time frames. Most people call them the ancient or old crystal skulls. These crystal skulls are completely activated, often have a lot of information downloaded, have witnessed many events and may have protocols that need to be followed to be able to access the stored information. It is not difficult to see and experience the diversity when we connect with the known ancient and old crystal skulls as we did in chapter 3.

With the start of our New Age—or the end of the old times as indicated by the Mayan calendar—our collective memory about crystal skulls seems to have been awakened. The interest in crystal skulls has led to the carving of many contemporary skulls. The number of these carvings is still increasing due to a growing interest in crystal skulls. The contemporary crystal skulls are wonderful tools to experience the phenomenon of crystal skulls.

By mentioning the contemporary crystal skulls, the story about the crystal skulls has reached the here and now. It is up to those who are interested in the crystal skulls to continue the story and to experience what the ancients must have experienced when they fully connected with the phenomenon of crystal skulls.

COLOR 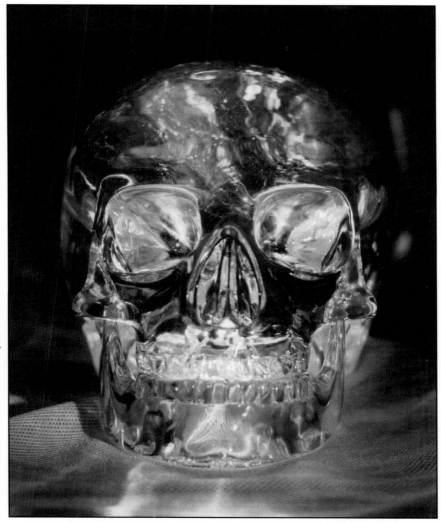 PLATES

Plate 1. The Mitchell-Hedges crystal skull.

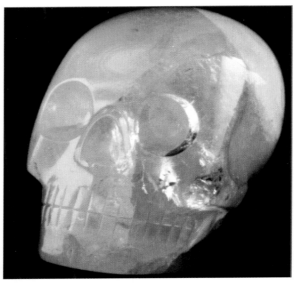

Photo © Jaap van Etten

Plate 2. Max, the Texas Skull, made from clear quartz, travels extensively with his caretaker, JoAnn Parks, allowing thousands of people to view and experience him.

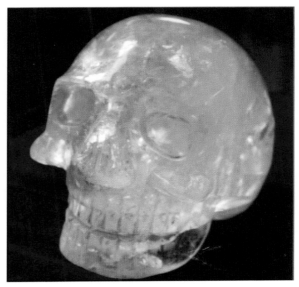

Photo © Cees Brouwer

Plate 3. ShaNaRa, a clear quartz skull, was found in 1995 during an excavation of a Mayan site in the state of Guerrero in Mexico.

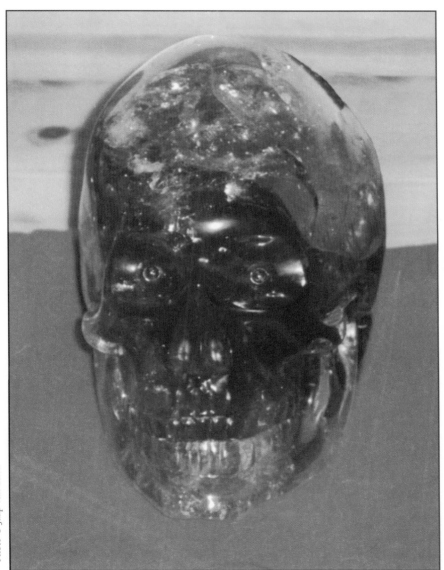

Plate 4. E.T., a smoky quartz skull, is slightly larger than a human skull, with a slightly pointed head and an overbite.

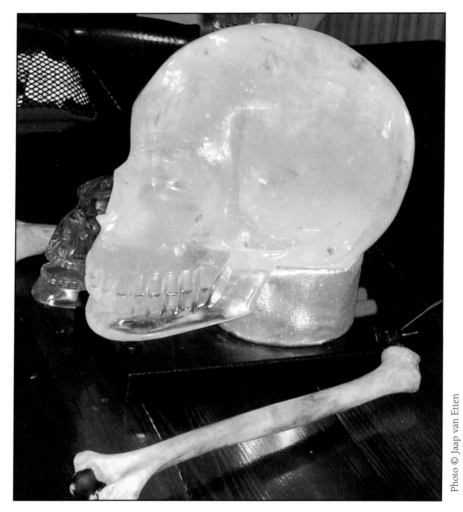

Photo © Jaap van Etten

Plate 5. Synergy, a large clear quartz crystal skull.

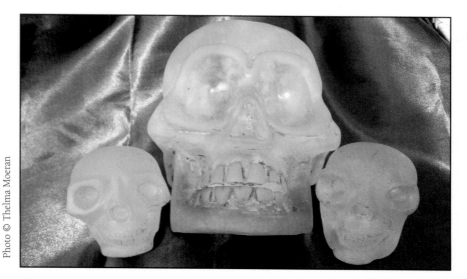

Plate 6. Three of the Himalayan Skulls: HeartStar (left), Golden Sister of the Moon (center) and Apollo 7 (right).

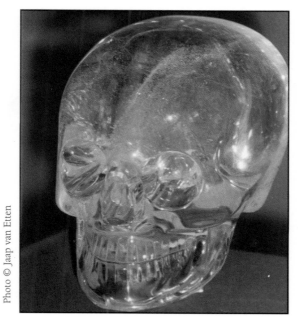

Plate 7. The British Skull, made from a single piece of clear quartz, is housed in the British Museum in London, England.

Photo © Thelma Moeran

Photo © Jaap van Etten

Photo © Amayra Hamilton

Plate 8. Ti (left) and Bet (right): two fully activated ancient/old crystal skulls from Tibet.

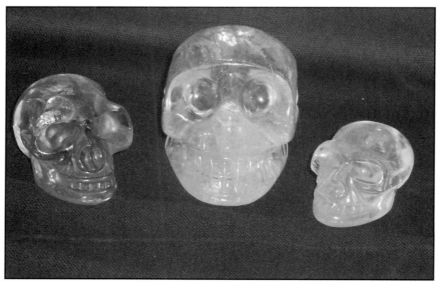

Photo © Jaap van Etten

Plate 9. Three fully activated crystal skulls from Nepal.

Photo © Amayra Hamilton

Plate 10. Group of contemporary crystal skulls from Amayra Hamilton.

Photo © Jaap van Etten

Plate 11. Loving crystal skulls are not only for humans.

Photo © Eric and Susan Youngman

Plate 12. A block of bishop jasper (4 PHF) about to be carved into a crystal skull.

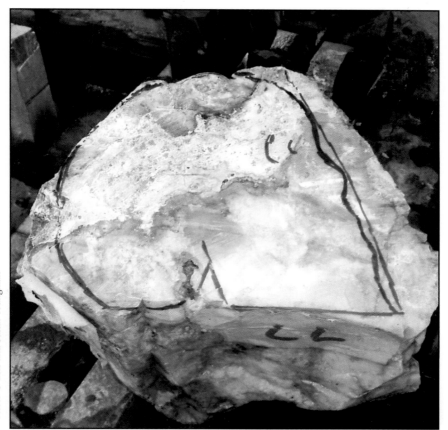

Plate 13. Outline the crystal skull on the rock (4 PHF).

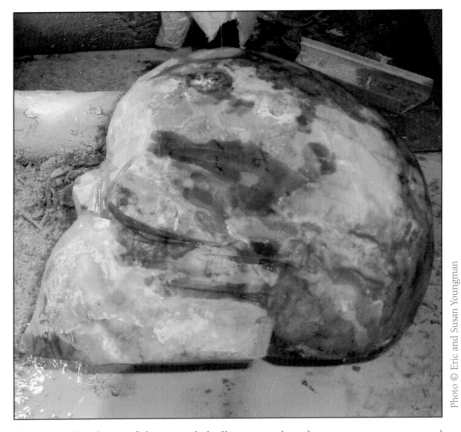

Photo © Eric and Susan Youngman

Plate 14. The shape of the crystal skull appears, but there are not yet eyes and other details (shift to 6 PHF).

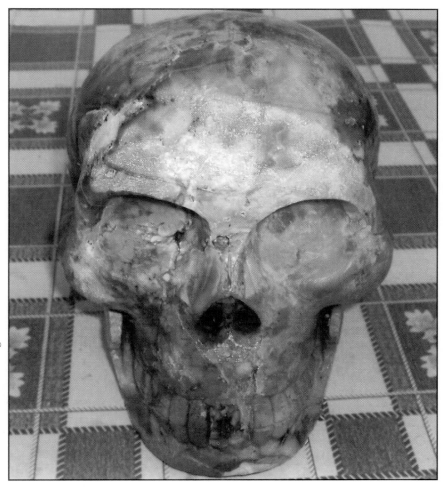

Plate 15. The final product: a crystal skull about eight inches (6 PHF).

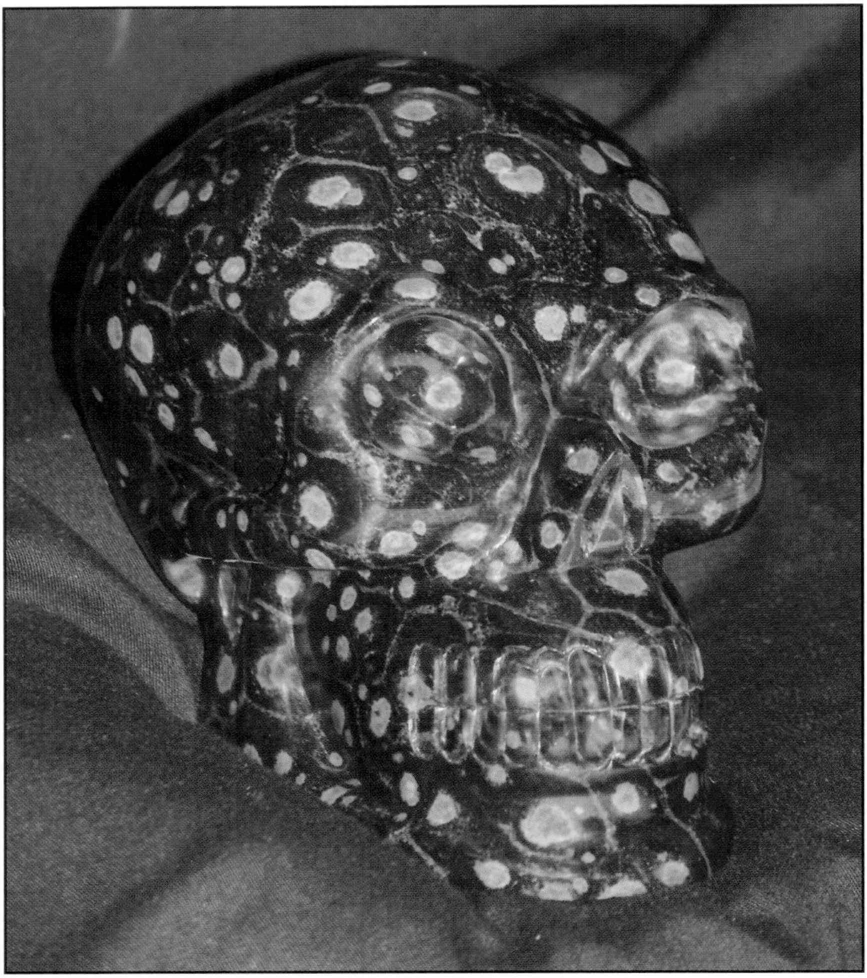

Plate 16. The largest nebula stone skull carved to date at six inches.

Photo © Amayra Hamilton

Plate 17. The location of the Sedona crystal skull portal at the base of the shoe-shaped rock.

Plate 18. Sam at the center of the Sedona crystal skull portal.

Plate 19. Sam during research on portals in Sedona.

Photo © Jaap van Etten

Photo © Amayra Hamilton

Plate 20. Our crystal skull family organized into the thirteen portal groups.

Plate 21. Myself at the center of the Mexico portal during the Mexico expedition in 1996.

Photo © Bas Meyer

Conclusion: The Future of the Crystal Skulls

hen we describe the function of crystal skulls in general and that of the different groups of crystal skulls in particular, we can to some degree predict the future of the work with crystal skulls. In a sense, this work will develop in a way that seems to be opposite to the development of the past. As humankind, we started with the original skulls. We then had the singing skulls, then the crystal skulls carved in ancient and old times, and now we have the contemporary skulls. We might call this process *involution*, where our awareness and abilities to work with crystal skulls have decreased. In our time, an increasing number of people are buying contemporary skulls, which has started the process of *evolution*. We are now expanding our consciousness again as we become more and more aware of the potentials we have always had. Our abilities are awakening again.

Many of the caretakers of contemporary crystal skulls do amazing work with them. While working and interacting with our crystal skulls, we deepen our connection with the crystal skulls in general. We begin to learn how to fully activate them. By sharing with each other, our understanding of crystal skulls accelerates. We are growing into a phase in which we will be able to access the information of the fully activated crystal skulls, those we call the old and the ancient ones. We are learning that there is no need to go into discussion regarding which one is older, because from the point of view of understanding and working with these crystal skulls, that is completely irrelevant.

The next step in this evolutionary line will be to sense the protocols that were used to program the information that is stored in many, if not all, of the ancient crystal skulls. Working with these fully programmed skulls prepares us for the next step: accessing the singing crystal skulls. The singing skulls work on a different level than the "talking" or fully activated skulls. This is the last step before we can access the original crystal skulls, which will allow us to access the information that will help us to truly shift our understanding and awareness of the universe we live in. It may be possible that the ability to fully access, understand and connect with the singing skulls will connect us straight with the original skulls. We will only know what happens when we are willing to participate in this evolutionary journey.

The journey I describe is the evolutionary journey of humankind. There may be individuals who will be ahead of the general evolution, and they will prepare the way. Several if not many of these people are magically attracted to the crystal skulls and feel that they resonate with these skulls in an intense way. It is a journey of the realization that we already have the knowledge and that the journey has already been completed—to realize that we already have made the connection. The only thing we need to do is to believe this is true. We are not separated from the knowledge of the original crystal skulls—we have chosen to forget that we already have that connection. The crystal skulls help us to realize this and offer the possibility to reconnect.

There is one more aspect of interacting with crystal skulls that I would like to mention. One of the reasons we have lost our connection with the Earth, with crystals and crystal skulls, and with many other subjects that are considered unscientific, is the choice to believe that our mind is more important than our feelings. Descartes once said, "Cogito, ergo sum" ("I think, therefore I am"), and this has had a tremendous impact on our modern society. We started to believe that what we think is truth. If it is not "logical," it cannot be true. Our view of the world is determined by what we think about the world, which in turn is based on what we have been taught. We follow the scientific and religious paradigms, and in these paradigms, there is no place for magic. We have lost the magical aspect of the world, and with that we have lost an important part of what the world is, for besides information, it is also personal experience. We believed in facts and logic based on what we know. Experiences that cannot be explained by the mind have no value.

We are now beginning to realize that this approach through the mind is a one-sided way to look at the world. We are beginning to allow ourselves to feel and sense again. Experiences are regaining value. Crystal skulls are tools that invite us to feel, to sense and to listen to what the energies are conveying to us, what they do with us and how they make us feel. The crystal skulls invite us to move from a masculine approach to the world (the world of the mind, of thinking and of action) to a feminine approach (connecting, feeling, sensing), with the purpose of integrating those two approaches into a new way to experience and connect with the world. The outer world is a reflection of our inner world. When we more fully experience the world, we will also more fully experience ourselves. This is what we are on Earth for: to express who we truly are. Only through experience will we understand what that means.

Endnotes

Author's note: Whenever I use direct quotes, they are always between quotation marks; they are literally taken from the source. But when the quotations come from audiotapes, what results is my interpretation of what I thought was on the tape. This is especially the case with Bashar.

Overview

1. When I was shown this information in meditation, I did not have the proper terms for this process. Later I found the terms I am using, which perfectly describe the processes, in Sandra Bowen, F.R. "Nick" Nocerino and Joshua Shapiro, *Mysteries of the Crystal Skulls Revealed* (Pacifica, CA: J&S Aquarian Networking, 1988).

2. Darryl Anka (Bashar), undated channeling, Los Angeles, California.

Chapter 1

1. Darryl Anka (Bashar), "Crystals and Electromagnetism," November 16, 1987, Encino, California, audiotape. For more information, see http://www.bashar.org/HOMEMAIN.html. (In the catalog, this channeling is called "Crystals.")

Chapter 2

1. Joshua Shapiro and DesyRainbow Roodnat-Shapiro, *Journeys of the Crystal Skull Explorers*, e-book. (See http://www.v-j-enterprises.com/cs.html for more information.) This e-book has been published in Dutch in a condensed form: *Kristallen Schedels, Een groot mysterie nader bekeken* (The Netherlands: Akasha Publishing, 2006).

2. The website for the Crystal Skull Festival in Holland in October 2006 still exists and forms the basis for announcements of new events (http://www.crystalskullevents.org).

3. This information was given in a private session with Bashar in Los Angeles on June, 23, 2007.

Chapter 3

1. The Mitchell-Hedges Skull is the crystal skull that has been given the most attention. Whenever a new article on crystal skulls appears, the Mitchell-Hedges Skull is featured. There are not many books on crystal skulls, but several of them feature this skull solely as their main topic. The following books focus on the Mitchell-Hedges Skull:

   * Sibley Morrill, *Ambrose Bierce, F.A. Mitchell-Hedges, and the Crystal Skull* (San Francisco: Cadleon Press, 1972).

   * Richard Garvin, *The Crystal Skull* (New York: Simon & Schuster, 1974).

   * Brian Hadley-James, ed., *The Skull Speaks Through Carole Davis* (Toronto: Amhrea Publishing, 1985).

   * Alice Bryant and Phyllis Galde, *The Message of the Crystal Skull: From Atlantis to the New Age* (St. Paul, MN: Llewellyn Publications, 1989).

   * Frank Dorland, *Holy Ice: Bridge to the Subconscious* (St. Paul, MN: Galde Press, 1992).

   Other books that contain important information on the Mitchell-Hedges Skull are:

   * Sandra Bowen, F.R. "Nick" Nocerino and Joshua Shapiro, *Mysteries of the Crystal Skulls Revealed* (Pacifica, CA: J&S Aquarian Networking, 1988).

   * Chris Morton, and Ceri Louise Thomas, *The Mystery of the Crystal Skulls: Unlocking the Secrets of the Past, Present, and Future*, second edition (Rochester, VT: Bear & Company, 2002).

   * Joshua Shapiro and DesyRainbow Roodnat-Shapiro, *Journeys of the Crystal Skull Explorers*, e-book. (See http://www.v-j-enterprises.com /cs.html for more information.)

2. Bowen, et al., *Mysteries of the Crystal Skulls Revealed*, 11.

3. Morton and Thomas, *The Mystery of the Crystal Skulls*, 210.

4. Bowen, et al., *Mysteries of the Crystal Skulls Revealed*, 34–36.

5. Ibid.

6. Ibid.

7. Ibid.

8. Ibid.

9. There are many articles about Max on the Internet. Max is also mentioned in the book: Morton and Thomas, *The Mystery of the Crystal Skulls*, 79–88, 212, 219, 220, 222–225, 326. Max is still traveling in the United States and also in Europe, and JoAnn Parks has written a booklet called, "The Story of Max, the Texas Crystal Skull" (1990). (This is a $4.00 booklet that can be bought through her: JoAnn Parks, PO Box 751261, Houston, Texas 77275-1261.)

10. Morton and Thomas, *The Mystery of the Crystal Skulls*, 223–224.

11. Ami, the Amethyst crystal skull, is mentioned in several books, such as Bowen, et al., *Mysteries of the Crystal Skulls Revealed*; Morton and Thomas, *The Mystery of the Crystal Skulls*, 93; and Shapiro and Shapiro, *Journeys of the Crystal Skull Explorers*, 44–49. There are also many references under "Amethyst crystal skull" on the Internet.

12. There is not much information about the Mayan Skull. It is mentioned in Bowen, et al., *Mysteries of the Crystal Skulls Revealed*; and in Shapiro and Shapiro, *Journeys of the Crystal Skull Explorers*, 83. Plus, there is some information on the Internet when you search for "Mayan Skull."

13. E.T. is mentioned in Morton and Thomas, *The Mystery of the Crystal Skulls*, 210; and in Shapiro and Shapiro, *Journeys of the Crystal Skull Explorers*, 49–54. The caretaker Joky van Dieten has her own website (http://www.jokys-peacemission.com/skulls.htm), but this skull is also mentioned on many crystal skull websites: type in search words "crystal skull E.T."

14. ShaNaRa is mentioned in Morton and Thomas, *The Mystery of the Crystal Skulls*, 222–225; and in N. Charles C. Pelton, "The Crystal

Skull Enigma," *Atlantis Rising* 10 (Winter 1997): 32–34, 65–66. (The Pelton article is also available on the Internet: http://www.atlantis-rising/issue10/ar10crystalskull.html.) There are also many websites that mention this crystal skull (search under "crystal skull ShaNaRa" or "Shanara").

15. Pelton, "The Crystal Skull Enigma," 64.

16. ShaNaRa and the British Museum research are mentioned in Morton and Thomas, *The Mystery of the Crystal Skulls*, 222–225.

17. N. Charles C. Pelton, *The Crystal Skulls: A Legacy of Past Civilizations or Prophets of our Future?* (Pinole, CA: Pelton Publications, 1997), 19. (Publication no longer available.)

18. There is not much information available about this crystal skull. Most is located on the website of the Crystal Awareness Institute of DaEl Walker: http://www.crystalawareness.com/crystalskulls/-index.html. Chuck Pelton also gives some information on this skull in *The Crystal Skulls*.

19. From the website of Crystal Awareness Institute of DaEl Walker: http://www.crystalawareness.com/crystal-skulls/index.html.

20. Pelton, *The Crystal Skulls*, 19.

21. Synergy and Sherry Whitfield have a website: http://www.crystal-skull.com. Synergy is also mentioned in Shapiro and Shapiro, *Journeys of the Crystal Skull Explorers*, 63–73.

22. The Himalayan skulls used to have their own website. Now they are spread out and there are several caretakers who do not (yet) have their own websites, with exception of HeartStar: http://www.astro-journeys.com/heartstar.html. On this website are also photos of Apollo7 and the crystal skull Golden Sister of the Moon. There still remains one website showing all the Himalayan skulls: http://www.greatdreams.com/himalayan/skull3.html.

23. This information was given in a personal session with Bashar in Los Angeles on March 19, 2007.

24. Much attention has been paid to the British Skull, also called the British Museum Skull. Several books dedicate many pages to the

skull, such as Bowen, et al., *Mysteries of the Crystal Skulls Revealed*; and Morton and Thomas, *The Mystery of the Crystal Skulls*. Also, Joshua Shapiro dedicates a chapter to this skull in *Journeys of the Crystal Skull Explorers*, 73–80. Many web pages on the Internet mention this skull as well (use the search words: "British skull").

25. Morton and Thomas, *The Mystery of the Crystal Skulls*, 221.

26. As one of the earlier discovered crystal skulls, the Paris Skull is mentioned in many books, such as Bowen, et al., *Mysteries of the Crystal Skulls Revealed*; and Morton and Thomas, *The Mystery of the Crystal Skulls*, 75–76, 100, 102, 104, 105, 108, 111, 112. It is also found on many websites (search "Paris crystal skull").

27. Pelton, *The Crystal Skulls*, 11; and Shapiro and Shapiro, *Journeys of the Crystal Skull Explorers*, 80–82.

28. Windsong has not received much attention, mostly because it has hardly come out. It is said that the caretaker Floyd Petri is writing a book on his experiences with Windsong.

29. Baby Luv, another skull of caretaker Joky van Dieten, has had less attention than E.T. It is mentioned on a few websites, most notably Joky's website: http://www.jokys-peacemission.com/skulls.htm.

30. There is very limited information available on Shui Ting Er. Again, see Joky van Dieten's website: http://www.jokys-peacemission.com/skulls.htm.

31. The Jesuit is more often mentioned and researched than the first two; still, there is not much written about it. Again see: http://www.jokys-peacemission.com/skulls.htm.

32. The only place Mansur, Oceana, Magnificent Fire and Clouds are mentioned is at http://www.jokys-peacemission.com/skulls.htm.

33. Ibid.

34. Ibid.

35. Ibid.

36. For more on Joky's peace mission, see her website: http://www.jokys-peacemission.com/skulls.htm.

37. The interview with Willaru Huayta can be found on http://www.v-j-enterprises.com/peruskul.html.

38. The only reference I have found for the Peru Skull is on the website: http://www.v-j-enterprises.com/peruskul.html. It is, however, a much talked-about skull, which is why I included it in this text.

39. More information about the two skulls of Susan Isabelle Boynton can be found on her website, http://www.Shambhalatemple.com, and in her soon-to-be-published book: Susan Isabelle, *The Global Assignment: Activate the Crystal Skulls: Fulfilling the Maya's Prophesies*. She also talks about these skulls in her other two books: *On Assignment with Adama: Mt. Shasta, Telos, Lemuria, and Sacred Earth Sites, Book I* (Bloomington, IN: AuthorHouse, 2005), and *Return the Goddess, the Lemurians Shall Come: Book II* (Bloomington, IN: AuthorHouse, 2007).

Chapter 4

1. There are many crystal shops that have crystal skulls for sale. Most of these crystal skulls come from a limited number of people who sell crystal skulls. Some of them select the material themselves, which they then send to carvers who give them the style they like. This is not the place to make an extensive list, but I would like to mention a few crystal skull sellers whom I have learned to respect.

    * Eric and Susan Youngman: Their website is http://www.soul2shine.com, and their email address is s2s@soul2shine.com. Eric and Susan themselves select the high-grade material that is used for the carving of the crystal skulls they sell. Many of our crystal skulls came from them.

    * Joe and MaryLee Swanson: We have also bought many of our crystal skulls from them. They have been selling crystal skulls for quite a while and get their material from different sources. Their email address is krystals@webtv.net.

* Sherry Whitfield Merrell: She sells crystal skulls via her and Synergy's website, http://www.crystalskull.net, and via her eBay store, http://stores.ebay.com/Blue-Star-Traders.
* Another way to find crystal skulls is via online auctions on eBay (http://www.ebay.com). Here, other sellers sell wonderful crystal skulls. We have bought crystal skulls from sellers at eBay, but we are less familiar with them than the sellers mentioned above.
2. Joshua Shapiro and DesyRainbow Roodnat-Shapiro, *Journeys of the Crystal Skull Explorers*, e-book. (See http://www.v-j-enterprises.com/cs.html for more information.)

Chapter 5

1. David Bohm has written many interesting books on the explicate and implicate orders. See *Wholeness and the Implicate Order* (New York: Routledge, 2002); and *The Undivided Universe* (New York: Routledge, 1995).
2. For more information on Resonance Field Imaging™, see the website of Innovation Technologies and Energy Medicine (ITEM): http://www.item-bioenergy.com/rfi/intro.html.
3. The term "copyrighted materials" is used by ITEM. What this means is, you need material that is copyrighted by them. You will receive these materials when you purchase the instruments and computer program that are needed to use the Resonance Field Imaging™.
4. The website on nebula stone is http://www.nebulastone.com. Nebula stone is mentioned in many crystal skull books.

Chapter 6

1. Research supporting this is available online on the Transcendental Meditation Program website: http://www.tm.org/charts/chart_46.html, under Scientific Research/Decreased Crime Rate in Cities. See also http://www.tm.org/charts/chart_46.html.

2. I have carried out extensive research on Earth energies, and I have studied and still study Earth energy lines and vortexes. Vortexes are places where Earth energies move in and/or out of the Earth. There are many different types of these vortexes. On the average, the optimal size of the vortexes of each type is similar all over the world. During my studies, it became apparent that the size of lines and vortexes in cities and in nature differ considerably. While in Taiwan, I compared vortexes of the same type that were located either in cities or in nature. In nature, the vortexes were around 80 percent optimal, but in cities they were only around 40 percent. In Western Europe, I have found the vortexes to be even more depleted. For example, in the Netherlands every square inch has been influenced by human beings and consequently the average size of the vortexes was between 20 to 30 percent, depending on the type of vortex. There, there is no longer a difference between city and nature. In Denmark, the situation was only slightly better (30 to 40 percent). In the Red Rock area of Sedona, Arizona, I have found the size of lines and vortexes to be similar to those of Taiwan in nature: 80 to 90 percent.

3. Joshua Shapiro and DesyRainbow Roodnat-Shapiro, *Journeys of the Crystal Skull Explorers*, e-book, 316–336. (See http://www.v-j-enterprises.com/cs.html for more information.)

4. Ibid, 331–332.

5. Ibid, 336–341.

6. Sandra Bowen, F.R. "Nick" Nocerino and Joshua Shapiro, *Mysteries of the Crystal Skulls Revealed* (Pacifica, CA: J&S Aquarian Networking, 1988): 26–27.

7. Ibid.

8. Again, see http://www.tm.org/charts/chart_46.htm (under Scientific Research/Decreased Crime Rate in Cities), or http://www.tm.org/charts/chart_46.html.

Chapter 7

1. Brian Hadley James, ed., *The Skull Speaks Through Carole Davis* (Toronto: Amhrea Publishing, 1985).

2. Ibid, 17, 23.

3. Kathleen Murray, *The Divine Spark of Creation: The Crystal Skull Speaks*, boxed gift set of book and images (England: Galactic Publications, 1998).

4. Ibid, 7.

5. Ibid, 8.

6. Ibid, back of cover of images.

7. Sandra Bowen, F.R. "Nick" Nocerino and Joshua Shapiro, *Mysteries of the Crystal Skulls Revealed* (Pacifica, CA: J&S Aquarian Networking, 1988).

8. Ibid, 157.

9. Ibid, 158–205.

10. Ibid, 160.

11. Ibid, 161.

12. Ibid, 163–167.

13. Ibid, 207.

14. Ibid, 208–216.

15. Ibid, 208–209.

16. Ibid, 209.

17. Ibid, 214.

18. Information on Monitor and Harvey Grady can be found at http://www.sedonaspirit.com. Books and transcripts are available through this website. Harvey Grady also has a newsletter available called *Explore!*, which publishes the transcripts of each weekly channeling.

19. Harvey Grady, "Monitor Readings Update," *Explore!*, Volume 1, Issue 7 (February 7, 2001): 5.

20. Ibid.

21. Ibid.

22. Ibid, 6.

23. Ibid.

24. Ibid.

25. This lecture is on a videotape and is part of the Lazaris Material. *Crystals: The Mystery & Magic of "Ancient One" Crystals & Crystal Skulls*, videocassette, directed by Michaell North (Orlando, FL: NPN Publishing, Inc., 1984). See also http://www.Lazaris.com.

26. Ibid.

27. Ibid.

28. Ibid.

29. Ibid.

30. Ibid.

31. Ibid.

32. Ibid.

33. Bashar has been channeled by Darryl Anka for more than twenty-one years. Many of the channelings are available on tape or even on DVD. See http://www.bashar.org.

Chapter 8

1. Kenneth Meadows, *The Medicine Way: A Shamanic Path to Self-Mastery*, reprint (Rockport, MA: Element Books, Ltd., 1993).

2. During a visit to Taiwan in 2005, I was brought to a place that is called a Pleiadian portal. According to written history, the Aborigines of Taiwan called this the place they communicated with the ancestors.

3. Meadows, *The Medicine Way*, 12–17.

4. Ibid, 13.

5. Ibid.

6. Sandra Bowen, F.R. "Nick" Nocerino and Joshua Shapiro, *Mysteries of the Crystal Skulls Revealed* (Pacifica, CA: J&S Aquarian Networking, 1988).

7. Bowen, et al., *Mysteries of the Crystal Skulls Revealed*, 214; and Chris Morton, and Ceri Louise Thomas, *The Mystery of the Crystal Skulls: Unlocking the Secrets of the Past, Present, and Future*, second edition (Rochester, VT: Bear & Company, 2002), 346.

8. Nicholas R. Mann, *Sedona: Sacred Earth* (Flagstaff, AZ: Light Technology Publishing, 2005), 87–88.

9. More information on Bryan de Flores and his work can be found at his website: http://www.bryandeflores.com. The crystal skull accelerators are no longer available as a separate set but only as part of a large book of his art titled *Masterworks: The Golden Age*, which is available on his website. A few are still available as separate images, also on his website.

10. Bowen, et al., *Mysteries of the Crystal Skulls Revealed*, 213–214.

11. Ibid, 214.

12. For articles on the activation of the Sedona Landscape Temple, see http://www.lemurantis.com/sedonalandscapetemple.html, and http://www.lemurantis.com/secondactivation.html.

Chapter 9

1. Sandra Bowen, F.R. "Nick" Nocerino and Joshua Shapiro, *Mysteries of the Crystal Skulls Revealed* (Pacifica, CA: J&S Aquarian Networking, 1988), 16, 21.

2. Chris Morton, and Ceri Louise Thomas, *The Mystery of the Crystal Skulls: Unlocking the Secrets of the Past, Present, and Future*, second edition (Rochester, VT: Bear & Company, 2002), 320–325.

3. Ibid.

4. Ibid.

5. Ibid.

6. Morton and Thomas, *The Mystery of the Crystal Skulls*, 323.

7. Morton and Thomas, *The Mystery of the Crystal Skulls*, 320–325.

8. Ibid.

9. Ibid, 342–352.

10. Ibid.

11. Ibid, 346–347.

12. Ibid, 243–253.

13. Ibid.

14. Ibid.

15. Lynne McTaggert, *The Field: The Quest for the Secret Force of the Universe* (New York: HarperCollins Publishers, 2002), 46–47.

16. Morton and Thomas, *The Mystery of the Crystal Skulls*, 251.

17. Ibid, 327–333.

18. Ibid.

19. Ibid.

20. Bowen, et al., *Mysteries of the Crystal Skulls Revealed*, 157–207.

21. Ibid.

22. Ibid, 161.

23. Ibid, 160.

24. Ibid, 163–171.

25. Ibid, 211.

26. Frank Dorland, *Holy Ice: Bridge to the Subconscious* (St. Paul, MN: Galde Press, 1992), 44–47.

27. Bowen, et al., *Mysteries of the Crystal Skulls Revealed*, 68–69.

Chapter 10

1. Books that describe the Platonic solids and also place them in a larger context of sacred geometry are:

   * Robert Lawlor, *Sacred Geometry: Philosophy and Practice* (London, England: Thames and Hudson, 1989).

   * Drunvalo Melchizedek, *The Ancient Secret of the Flower of Life, Volume 1* (Flagstaff, AZ: Light Technology Publishing, 1999).

   * Richard Dannelley, *Sedona: Beyond the Vortex* (Sedona, AZ: The Vortex Society, 1995).

Much basic information on the Platonic solids is also available on the Internet.

2. This information is summarized on the Internet in an article "Is the Universe a Dodecahedron?" (http://physicsworld.com/cws/article/news/18368). The article was originally published by Jean-Pierre Luminet, Jeffrey R. Weeks, Alain Riazuelo, Roland Lehoucq and Jean-Philippe Uzan, "Dodecahedral Space Topology as an Explanation for Weak Wide-Angle Temperature Correlations in the Cosmic Microwave Background," *Nature* 425 (October 9, 2003): 593.

3. Michael Talbot, *The Holographic Universe* (New York: HarperCollins Publishers Ltd., 1996).

Chapter 11

1. Darryl Anka (Bashar), undated channeling, Los Angeles, California.

2. Drunvalo Melchizedek, *The Ancient Secret of the Flower of Life, Volume 1* (Flagstaff, AZ: Light Technology Publishing, 1999), 168–169.

3. Sandra Bowen, F.R. "Nick" Nocerino and Joshua Shapiro, *Mysteries of the Crystal Skulls Revealed* (Pacifica, CA: J&S Aquarian Networking, 1988), 170, 179; and Chris Morton, and Ceri Louise Thomas, *The Mystery of the Crystal Skulls: Unlocking the Secrets of the Past, Present, and Future*, second edition (Rochester, VT: Bear & Company, 2002), 330.

4. Kathleen Murray, *The Divine Spark of Creation: The Crystal Skull Speaks* (England: Galactic Publications, 1998), 149–244.

5. Ibid, 236.

6. Ibid, 149–244.

7. Otto Muck, *The Secret of Atlantis* (New York: Pocket Books, 1976), 9.

8. Jamie Sams, *The Thirteen Original Clan Mothers: Your Sacred Path to Discovering the Gifts, Talents, and Abilities of the Feminine* (San Francisco: HarperOne, 1994), 279.

9. Bowen, et al., *Mysteries of the Crystal Skulls Revealed*, 170–178, 213–214.

Bibliography

Anka, Darryl (Bashar). "Crystals and Electromagnetism." November 16, 1987. Encino, California. Audiotape.

Bentov, Itzhak. *Stalking the Wild Pendulum: On the Mechanics of Consciousness.* Rochester, VT: Destiny Books, 1988.

Bohm, David. *The Undivided Universe.* New York: Routledge, 1995.

_____. *Wholeness and the Implicate Order.* New York: Routledge, 2002.

Bowen, Sandra, F.R. "Nick" Nocerino and Joshua Shapiro. *Mysteries of the Crystal Skulls Revealed.* Pacifica, CA: J&S Aquarian Networking, 1988.

Bryant, Alice, and Phyllis Galde. *The Message of the Crystal Skull: From Atlantis to the New Age.* St. Paul, MN: Llewellyn Publications, 1989.

Dannelley, Richard. *Sedona: Beyond the Vortex.* Sedona, AZ: The Vortex Society, 1995.

Dorland, Frank. *Holy Ice: Bridge to the Subconscious.* St. Paul, MN: Galde Press, 1992.

Garvin, Richard. *The Crystal Skull.* New York: Simon & Schuster, 1974.

Grady, Harvey. "Monitor Readings Update." *Explore!,* Volume 1, Issue 7 (February 7, 2001), 5–6.

Hadley-James, Brian, ed. *The Skull Speaks Through Carole Davis.* Toronto: Amhrea Publishing, 1985.

Isabelle, Susan. *On Assignment with Adama: Mt. Shasta, Telos, Lemuria, and Sacred Earth Sites, Book I.* Bloomington, IN: AuthorHouse, 2005.

_____. *Return the Goddess, the Lemurians Shall Come: Book II.* Bloomington, IN: AuthorHouse, 2007.

_____. *The Global Assignment: Activate the Crystal Skulls: Fulfilling the Maya's Prophesies.* Publication pending.

Lawlor, Robert. *Sacred Geometry: Philosophy and Practice.* London, England: Thames and Hudson, 1989.

The Lazaris Material. *Crystals: The Mystery & Magic of "Ancient One" Crystals & Crystal Skulls.* Videocassette. Directed by Michaell North. Orlando, FL: NPN Publishing, Inc., 1984.

Luminet, Jean Pierre, Jeffrey R. Weeks, Alain Riazuelo, Roland Lehoucq and Jean-Philippe Uzan. "Dodecahedral Space Topology as an Explanation for Weak Wide-

Angle Temperature Correlations in the Cosmic Microwave Background." *Nature* 425 (October 9, 2003): 593.

Mann, Nicholas R. *Sedona: Sacred Earth*. Flagstaff, AZ: Light Technology Publishing, 2005.

McTaggert, Lynne. *The Field: The Quest for the Secret Force of the Universe*. New York: HarperCollins Publishers, 2002.

Meadows, Kenneth. *The Medicine Way: A Shamanic Path to Self-Mastery*. Reprint. Rockport, MA: Element Books, Ltd., 1993.

Melchizedek, Drunvalo. *The Ancient Secret of the Flower of Life, Volume 1*. Flagstaff, AZ: Light Technology Publishing, 1999.

Morrill, Sibley. *Ambrose Bierce, F.A. Mitchell-Hedges, and the Crystal Skull*. San Francisco: Cadleon Press, 1972.

Morton, Chris, and Ceri Louise Thomas. *The Mystery of the Crystal Skulls: Unlocking the Secrets of the Past, Present, and Future*. Second edition. Rochester, VT: Bear & Company, 2002.

Muck, Otto. *The Secret of Atlantis*. New York: Pocket Books, 1976.

Murray, Kathleen. *The Divine Spark of Creation: The Crystal Skull Speaks*. Boxed gift set of book and images. England: Galactic Publications, 1998.

Parks, JoAnn. "The Story of Max, the Texas Crystal Skull." 1990. (This is a $4.00 booklet that can be bought through her: JoAnn Parks, PO Box 751261, Houston, Texas 77275-1261.)

Pelton, N. Charles C. *The Crystal Skulls: A Legacy of Past Civilizations or Prophets of our Future?* Pinole, CA: Pelton Publications, 1997. (Publication no longer available.)

_____. "The Crystal Skull Enigma." *Atlantis Rising* 10 (Winter 1997): 32–34, 65–66.

Sams, Jamie. *The Thirteen Original Clan Mothers: Your Sacred Path to Discovering the Gifts, Talents, and Abilities of the Feminine*. San Francisco: HarperOne, 1994.

Shapiro, Joshua, and DesyRainbow Roodnat-Shapiro. *Journeys of the Crystal Skull Explorers*. E-book (http://www.v-j-enterprises.com/cs.html).

Talbot, Michael. *The Holographic Universe*. New York: HarperCollins Publishers Ltd., 1996.

Webb-De Sisto, Marion. *Crystal Skulls: Emissaries of Healing and Sacred Wisdom*. Philadelphia: Xlibris Corporation, 2002.

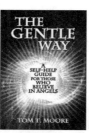
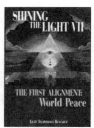

Publishing Presents

Plus Hundreds More!

A New Formula For Creation

Judith Moore

This book brings an inspiring positive message regarding the future of our planet. Earth is experiencing the Shift of the Ages, a time marked by massive Earth changes and social upheaval. This is foretold in many prophecies, including Hopi prophecies and the biblical Revelations. They warn that raising consciousness is the only way to avert a massive cataclysm.

$16.95 Softcover, 186 p. ISBN: 1-891824-57-0

Living in the Heart
(With CD)

Drunvalo Melchizedek

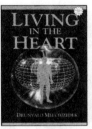

This is a book of remembering. You have always had this place within your heart, and it is still there now. It existed before creation, and it will exist even after the last star shines its brilliant light. This book is written with the least amount of words possible to convey the meaning and to keep the integrity of the essence of this experience. The images are purposefully simple. It is written from the heart, not the mind.

$25.00 Softcover, 120 p. ISBN: 1-891824-43-0

Ancient Secret of the Flower of Life *Vol. I*

Drunvalo Melchizedek

Once, all life in the universe knew the Flower of Life as the creation pattern —the geometrical design leading us into and out of physical existence. Sacred Geometry is the form beneath our being and points to a divine order in our reality. We can follow that order from the invisible atom to the infinite stars, finding ourselves at each step.

$25.00 Softcover, 228 p. ISBN: 1-891824-17-1

Change Your Encodements, Your DNA, Your Life!

Amma through
Cathy Chapman

The first part of this book discusses what you call love. Love is the most powerful energy. The second part contains powerful techniques for working with your DNA encodements. The third part contains what some call predictions, which are nothing more than my reading and interpretation of the energy at the time when the energy was read.

$16.95 Softcover, 303 p. ISBN: 1-891824-52-X

Animal Souls Speak
Explorer Race Series

Robert Shapiro

Welcome to the footsteps of the loving beings (animals) who support you, who wish to reveal more about themselves to you and who welcome you, not only to planet Earth, but more specifically to the pathway of self-discovery. The animal world will speak through elders, since that way they can include knowledge and wisdom about their home planets. Each animal brings a wonderous gift to share with humanity—enjoy it!

$29.95 Softcover, 610 p. ISBN: 1-891824-50-3

Ancient Secret of the Flower of Life *Vol. II*

Drunvalo Melchizedek

Drunvalo shares the instructions for the Mer-Ka-Ba meditation, step-by-step techniques for the re-creation of the energy field of the evolved human. From the pyramids and mysteries of Egypt to the new race of Indigo children, Drunvalo presents the sacred geometries of the Reality and the subtle energies that shape our world.

$25.00 Softcover, 477 p. ISBN: 1-891824-21-X

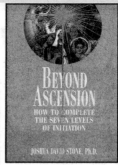

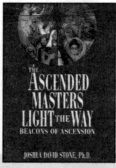

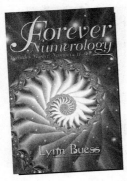

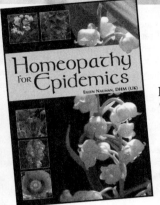

THE EXPLORER RACE SERIES

ZOOSH AND HIS FRIENDS THROUGH ROBERT SHAPIRO

THE SERIES: Humans—creators-in-training—have a purpose and destiny so heartwarmingly, profoundly glorious that it is almost unbelievable from our present dimensional perspective. Humans are great lightbeings from beyond this creation, gaining experience in dense physicality. This truth about the great human genetic experiment of the Explorer Race and the mechanics of creation is being revealed for the first time by Zoosh and his friends through superchannel Robert Shapiro. These books read like adventure stories as we follow the clues from this creation that we live in out to the Council of Creators and beyond.

❶ THE EXPLORER RACE

You individuals reading this are truly a result of the genetic experiment on Earth. You are beings who uphold the principles of the Explorer Race. The information in this book is designed to show you who you are and give you an evolutionary understanding of your past that will help you now. The key to empowerment in these days is to not know everything about your past, but to know what will help you now. Your number-one function right now is your status of Creator apprentice, which you have achieved through years and lifetimes of sweat. You are constantly being given responsibilities by the Creator that would normally be things that Creator would do. The responsibility and the destiny of the Explorer Race is not only to explore, but to create. 574 P. $25.00 ISBN 0-929385-38-1

❷ ETs and the EXPLORER RACE

In this book, Robert channels Joopah, a Zeta Reticulan now in the ninth dimension who continues the story of the great experiment—the Explorer Race—from the perspective of his civilization. The Zetas would have been humanity's future selves had not humanity re-created the past and changed the future. 237 P. $14.95 ISBN 0-929385-79-9

❸ EXPLORER RACE: ORIGINS and the NEXT 50 YEARS

This volume has so much information about who we are and where we came from—the source of male and female beings, the war of the sexes, the beginning of the linear mind, feelings, the origin of souls—it is a treasure trove. In addition, there is a section that relates to our near future—how the rise of global corporations and politics affects our future, how to use benevolent magic as a force of creation and how we will go out to the stars and affect other civilizations. Astounding information. 339 P. $14.95 ISBN 0-929385-95-0

❹ EXPLORER RACE: CREATORS and FRIENDS
The MECHANICS of CREATION

Now that you have a greater understanding of who you are in the larger sense, it is necessary to remind you of where you came from, the true magnificence of your being. You must understand that you are creators-in-training, and yet you were once a portion of Creator. One could certainly say, without being magnanimous, that you are still a portion of Creator, yet you are training for the individual responsibility of being a creator, to give your Creator a coffee break. This book will allow you to understand the vaster qualities and help you remember the nature of the desires that drive any creator, the responsibilities to which a creator must answer, the reaction a creator must have to consequences and the ultimate reward of any creator. 435 P. $19.95 ISBN 1-891824-01-5

❺ EXPLORER RACE: PARTICLE PERSONALITIES

All around you in every moment you are surrounded by the most magical and mystical beings. They are too small for you to see as single individuals, but in groups you know them as the physical matter of your daily life. Particles who might be considered either atoms or portions of atoms consciously view the vast spectrum of reality yet also have a sense of personal memory like your own linear memory. These particles remember where they have been and what they have done in their infinitely long lives. Some of the particles we hear from are Gold, Mountain Lion, Liquid Light, Uranium, the Great Pyramid's Capstone, This Orb's Boundary, Ice and Ninth-Dimensional Fire. 237 P. $14.95 ISBN 0-929385-97-7

❻ EXPLORER RACE and BEYOND

With a better idea of how creation works, we go back to the Creator's advisers and receive deeper and more profound explanations of the roots of the Explorer Race. The liquid Domain and the Double Diamond portal share lessons given to the roots on their way to meet the Creator of this universe, and finally the roots speak of their origins and their incomprehensibly long journey here. 360 P. $14.95 ISBN 1-891824-06-6

THE EXPLORER RACE SERIES

ZOOSH AND HIS FRIENDS THROUGH ROBERT SHAPIRO

⑦ EXPLORER RACE: The COUNCIL of CREATORS

The thirteen core members of the Council of Creators discuss their adventures in coming to awareness of themselves and their journeys on the way to the Council on this level. They discuss the advice and oversight they offer to all creators, including the Creator of this local universe. These beings are wise, witty and joyous, and their stories of Love's Creation create an expansion of our concepts as we realize that we live in an expanded, multiple-level reality. 237 P. $14.95 ISBN 1-891824-13-9

⑧ EXPLORER RACE and ISIS

This is an amazing book! It has priestess training, Shamanic training, Isis's adventures with Explorer Race beings—before Earth and on Earth—and an incredibly expanded explanation of the dynamics of the Explorer Race. Isis is the prototypal loving, nurturing, guiding feminine being, the focus of feminine energy. She has the ability to expand limited thinking without making people with limited beliefs feel uncomfortable. She is a fantastic storyteller, and all of her stories are teaching stories. If you care about who you are, why you are here, where you are going and what life is all about—pick up this book. You won't lay it down until you are through, and then you will want more. 317 P. $14.95 ISBN 1-891824-11-2

⑨ EXPLORER RACE and JESUS

The core personality of that being known on the Earth as Jesus, along with his students and friends, describes with clarity and love his life and teaching two thousand years ago. He states that his teaching is for all people of all races in all countries. Jesus announces here for the first time that he and two others, Buddha and Mohammed, will return to Earth from their place of being in the near future, and a fourth being, a child already born now on Earth, will become a teacher and prepare humanity for their return. So heartwarming and interesting, you won't want to put it down. 354 P. $16.95 ISBN 1-891824-14-7

⑩ EXPLORER RACE: Earth History and Lost Civilization

Speaks of Many Truths and Zoosh, through Robert Shapiro, explain that planet Earth, the only water planet in this solar system, is on loan from Sirius as a home and school for humanity, the Explorer Race. Earth's recorded history goes back only a few thousand years, its archaeological history a few thousand more. Now this book opens up as if a light was on in the darkness, and we see the incredible panorama of brave souls coming from other planets to settle on different parts of Earth. We watch the origins of tribal groups and the rise and fall of civilizations, and we can begin to understand the source of the wondrous diversity of plants, animals and humans that we enjoy here on beautiful Mother Earth. 310 P. $14.95 ISBN 1-891824-20-1

⑪ EXPLORER RACE: ET VISITORS SPEAK

Even as you are searching the sky for extraterrestrials and their spaceships, ETs are here on planet Earth—they are stranded, visiting, exploring, studying the culture, healing the Earth of trauma brought on by irresponsible mining or researching the history of Christianity over the past two thousand years. Some are in human guise, and some are in spirit form. Some look like what we call animals as they come from the species' home planet and interact with their fellow beings—those beings that we have labeled cats or cows or elephants. Some are brilliant cosmic mathematicians with a sense of humor; they are presently living here as penguins. Some are fledgling diplomats training for future postings on Earth when we have ET embassies here. In this book, these fascinating beings share their thoughts, origins and purposes for being here. 350 P. $14.95 ISBN 1-891824-28-7

⑫ EXPLORER RACE: Techniques for GENERATING SAFETY

Wouldn't you like to generate safety so you could go wherever you need to go and do whatever you need to do in a benevolent, safe and loving way for yourself? Learn safety as a radiated environment that will allow you to gently take the step into the new timeline, into a benevolent future and away from a negative past. 208 P. $9.95 ISBN 1-891824-26-0

Phone: 928-526-1345 or 1-800-450-0985 • Fax 928-714-1132

. . . or use our online bookstore at www.lighttechnology.com

Shamanic Secrets Mastery Series

Speaks of Many Truths and Reveals the Mysteries through Robert Shapiro

This book explores the heart and soul connection between humans and Mother Earth. Through that intimacy, miracles of healing and expanded awareness can flourish. To heal the planet and be healed as well, we can lovingly extend our energy selves out to the mountains and rivers and intimately bond with the Earth. Gestures and vision can activate our hearts to return us to a healthy, caring relationship with the land we live on. The character of some of Earth's most powerful features is explored and understood, with exercises given to connect us with those places. As we project our love and healing energy there, we help the Earth to heal from human destruction of the planet and its atmosphere. Dozens of photographs, maps and drawings assist the process in twenty-five chapters, which cover the Earth's more critical locations.

498 p. $19.95 ISBN 1-891824-12-0

Learn to understand the sacred nature of your own physical body and some of the magnificent gifts it offers you. When you work with your physical body in these new ways, you will discover not only its sacredness, but how it is compatible with Mother Earth, the animals, the plants, even the nearby planets, all of which you now recognize as being sacred in nature. It is important to feel the value of oneself physically before one can have any lasting physical impact on the world. If a physical energy does not feel good about itself, it will usually be resolved; other physical or spiritual energies will dissolve it because it is unnatural. The better you feel about your physical self when you do the work in the previous book as well as this one and the one to follow, the greater and more lasting will be the benevolent effect on your life, on the lives of those around you and ultimately on your planet and universe.

576 p. $25.00 ISBN 1-891824-29-5

Spiritual mastery encompasses many different means to assimilate and be assimilated by the wisdom, feelings, flow, warmth, function and application of all beings in your world that you will actually contact in some way. A lot of spiritual mastery has been covered in different bits and pieces throughout all the books we've done. My approach to spiritual mastery, though, will be as grounded as possible in things that people on Earth can use— but it won't include the broad spectrum of spiritual mastery, like levitation and invisibility. I'm trying to teach you things that you can actually use and benefit from. My life is basically going to represent your needs, and it gets out the secrets that have been held back in a storylike fashion, so that it is more interesting."

—Speaks of Many Truths through Robert Shapiro

768 p. $29.95 ISBN 1-891824-58-9

Phone: 928-526-1345 or 1-800-450-0985 • Fax 928-714-1132

. . . or use our online bookstore at www.lighttechnology.com